# THE FUTURE
## ·IS NOW·

## By J. Krishnamurti

# THE FUTURE
# ·IS NOW·

*Last Talks in India*

# J. KRISHNAMURTI

1817

HARPER & ROW, PUBLISHERS, SAN FRANCISCO

New York, Cambridge, Philadelphia, St. Louis
London, Singapore, Sydney, Tokyo

FIRST U.S. EDITION.
Originally published in England by Victor Gollancz, Ltd.

**Library of Congress Cataloging-in-Publication Data**

Krishnamurti, J. (Jiddu), 1895-
  The future is now.

  "Originally published in England by Victor Gollancz"—
T.p. verso.
  I. Title.
B5134.K753F86   1989      181'.4      88-45657
ISBN 0-06-250484-3

89  90  91  92  93  RRD  10  9  8  7  6  5  4  3  2  1

# CONTENTS

# INTRODUCTION

IT WAS KRISHNAMURTI'S last journey to India. He had
already stated at Saanen, Switzerland, that there would not
be any more talks there; and he had written to a friend:

We have had the most marvellous four days of weather,
sunny every day and the valley is telling us goodbye.

During the last talk at Saanen he retold the story of
Nachiketa, the boy who had been sent to the house of Death
for asking too many questions. It was an ancient Indian tale,
from the Kathopanishad, but Krishnamurti's version was
different — more romantic, set in an ideal time when men
kept their word and periodically gave away what they had
accumulated. These details are not in the original, which
does not have a romantic tone.

Krishnamurti's Nachiketa is full of impossible questions;
he is naive, but sufficiently astute to reject the temptations
Death offered with a simple observation, 'You will be at the
end of it. You will always be at the end of everything.'

Except that he was nearly 91, Krishnamurti was not very
different from the Nachiketa he described. He had
Nachiketa's gift for turning every occasion into a question,
even a boon; he had Nachiketa's easy way with death; and he
had Nachiketa's innocent generosity.

Krishnamurti's father in his reminiscences, recorded soon
after Krishnamurti had been brought into the fold of the
Theosophical Society, described an innocent generosity his
son never lost:

In the morning when beggars come to the house, it is our
custom to send out to them a cup or bowl of unboiled rice,
and we distribute it to the hands outheld in turn, until the
cup is empty. My wife would send Krishna out to give
alms, and the little fellow would come back for more,
saying he had poured it all into one man's bag. Then his
mother would go with him and teach him how to give to
each.

In later life, the innocent man and the sage lived together.
The man had come to India in October 1985 after talking at
Saanen and at Brockwood Park, England, to say goodbye to
the familiar landscape, to the people he had known and to
places he had nurtured. He had also come to set his house in
order.

Large educational institutions had grown at Rishi Valley
and Rajghat on land which had been bought for his use by
Mrs Annie Besant in the twenties. There were schools in
Bangalore, Madras and Bombay, dedicated to exploring his
teachings in an educational context. All these educational
institutions were part of the Krishnamurti Foundation,
India, a registered body of which he was president. Vasanta
Vihar, a house at Adyar in Madras, was the headquarters
of the Foundation and the address he used on his passport
where it said home address. There were foundations in
England and America also with well established educational
institutions.

Krishnamurti was also the man who in 1929 had dissolved
the Order of the wealthy organization which had grown
around him since 1909, when he had been 'discovered' by
the Theosophists. Then he had declared 'Truth cannot be
organized,' and relinquished the properties which went with
this organization.

The seeming contradiction between the man who rejects
spiritual organizations and the man who at the end of his life

finds himself at the head of several was resolved as long ago as 1929, when he ended that famous speech dissolving the Order:

> But those who desire to understand, who are looking to find that which is eternal, without beginning and end, will walk together with greater intensity, will be a danger to everything which is unessential, to unrealities, to shadows. And they will concentrate, they will become the flame, because they understand. *Such a body we must create*, and that is my purpose. Because of that true friendship . . . there will be real cooperation on the part of each one. And this not because of authority.

Krishnamurti's passionate concern, especially as he grew older and concerned about the health of the organizations he had himself established, was to create such a body of friends. At the same time his standards for friendship remained exacting: friendship could not flourish where there was envy, comparison, possessiveness. Only an abiding goodness, he believed, could hold people together. And the fruits of goodness were magical.

Sitting at the breakfast table one morning at Rishi Valley in the winter of 1984, in the middle of a trivial conversation, he asked us, 'If an angel told you that you could have anything you wanted for this place, what would you ask for?'

We mentioned several things — water, a new culture, a new mind — half-heartedly, knowing that our answers had been trotted out to satisfy the moment, knowing that they would be brushed aside. He did just that and continued, 'When we came here in 1926 our intention was to establish places for the enlightenment of man. Is this happening here?'

Again it was a difficult question; we admitted it was not happening.

'Is Rishi Valley then exactly like the world outside?' We said that it was a microcosm — we had the same problems on a smaller scale.

'Answer carefully,' he said. 'The outside world is war, deep resentment, strife, envy. Do you have these here? In you?'

We replied that though these things were not active in us, the seeds were there, and, 'given the situation, we might be capable of that also.'

He asked us if we could wipe all that out.

'If we wiped that out, would the angel give us what we want?'

He said simply, 'Yes.'

Krishnamurti arrived in New Delhi from London on the 25 October and proceeded shortly thereafter to Varanasi.* Aravindan, the noted film maker from Kerala, was finishing *The Seer Who Walks Alone*, based on Krishnamurti's life. In early November, with winter just setting in, Rajghat, in Varanasi, provided the framework for his film, with shots of the lone fisherman casting his net on a placid river; a bird flying in a wide arc over space which was both sky and river; and the setting sun becoming a halo for the sage who said: 'Man is not the measure of himself.'

Krishnamurti walked with Aravindan along the ancient pilgrim's path, now asphalted and much abused by lorries, as it led to the banks of the Varuna. He went across the temporary bamboo bridge to the other shore where the pilgrim's path, now narrow and dusty, surrounded by winter wheat, offered a glinting view of the Ganga [Ganges] and continued on to Sarnath. Here the Buddha had first preached his sermon 2,500 years ago. Aravindan's camera caught Krishnamurti's return journey across the bridge with the boatman who ferried men and animals to the other shore of the river during the monsoon when the bridge was down.

* The old name for Benares by which it is now known.

There was another path he walked every day, even when his legs had begun to fail him — along the winding path of the school campus, past the amphitheatre where students of the Vasanta College had recently performed a play on the life of the Buddha. The path ended in a steep flight of steps below which lay the circular playground and, set apart on one side with a wire fence, a mosque with its lounging caretaker. Along a ridge at the bottom of the steps a narrow path led off to the officers' graveyard,* long in disuse, and the site now of guest cottages for the new centre to be set up for those seriously interested in studying Krishnamurti's teachings.

Krishnamurti circled round the playground several times with friends, talking of many things, but chiefly of the questions which were of vital concern to him now: What would happen to the many institutions he had established? Would they fly apart without someone to hold them together? What was the future of the Foundations? And every time he completed a circle, he would greet the caretaker of the mosque, not wanting him to feel isolated, cut off.

The journey back, up that steep flight of steps, was a source of anxiety for his friends — they were never sure whether he would make it to the top without falling. Once somebody, a woman, offered him her hand. And with his usual gallantry he took it for a moment, remarked that he wanted to hold her hand, but 'I don't ever want to become dependent, on anybody.' The last was said with an emphasis and a look which gave her a sense of the unknown silence which lay ahead.

It was not during these walks but upstairs in his bedroom that he spoke of sacred places as places of learning, and therefore, by definition, beyond the compass of ritual, of churches, temples and mosques. He said that a place was

* Rajghat had been a British fort.

sacred if it was marked by three characteristics — by the religiosity of people who lived there, by the pilgrims who came there for the sake of truth, and by its ability to sustain life.

Mrs Besant was very much in Krishnamurti's mind that winter in Rajghat. On 6 November, he was invited to the Theosophical Lodge at Kamaccha, an invitation he accepted. He went to Mrs Besant's old house, 'Shantikunj'. With the late afternoon sun flooding in, he went round the old house. He sat on the great *chowki* where Mrs Besant worked and rested during the day. To those who had known Mrs Besant and Krishnamurti during those early days, it was an emotional moment. To one who had lived through that time, it was a day of great blessing: 'The son visits his mother's home, after an interval of 45 years. Perhaps to say goodbye.' But when someone asked Krishnamurti if he remembered the place, his reply was simple: 'It is long past — but it seems I did live here.'

The festival of Diwali came on the 16 November and Krishnamurti spent the evening with his friends watching a display of fireworks across from his house on the paved terrace high above the Ganges. As the sparklers and *kotis* scattered many coloured stars into the moonless sky, the city of Varanasi glowed in the distance. Krishnamurti then climbed onto the balcony of his house to relight the lamps that had gone out and to admire the view. It was an elegant evening when sanctity hung like a curtain over Rajghat.

There was more entertainment — an evening of Vedic chanting by the local Brahmins attached to the temple schools and the household of Maharaja of Varanasi; music on the *Shahanai Santoor* and an hour of *Kathak* danced by Aditi Mangaldas.

On 7 November, Krishnamurti began a series of discussions with a group of Buddhist scholars — Sanskritists and Tibetologists — that had gathered around him since the early seventies. They were part of a long tradition of scholars who had preserved a religious tradition for thousands of years through scholarly activities, strenuous philosophical debate and inward search.

Among them was Pandit Jagannath Upadhyaya. Panditji, as we called him, was engaged in producing a critical edition of the *Kalachakratantra*, a Mahayana text which dealt with the teaching of the Bodhisattva Maitreya. Composed some time between the ninth and the eleventh centuries, the text represented a much older tradition of wisdom, which Panditji once had described as 'the ancestry of man'. Panditji's description had struck a chord in Krishnamurti who had modified the phrase to say, 'the ancestry of insight'.

Rinpoche Sandong of the Tibetan Institute at Sarnath, Professors Krishnanath and Ram Shankar Tripathi, both based at local educational institutions, were also present on the occasion.

Before this assembly of scholars, Krishnamurti raised two questions: 'Is there something sacred, something long lasting . . . in India, in this part of the world?' and, 'If it is there, why is this part of the world so corrupt?'

Krishnamurti answered both the questions he had posed. He answered the first question towards the end of the discussion when several issues had been raised and set aside, and the assembly sat quiet. H answered the second question on the basis of a generalized observation: 'Self-interest is the door that shuts the other out.' The concept of self-interest was for Krishnamurti both very wide as well as elastic; it included in its net the impulse behind organized religion.

On the 11th, Krishnamurti posed a third question: 'Where does self-interest end and the other begin?' And though he returned to the question at least twice in the course of the discussion, he did not answer it. He left it as an eternal question, a doubt which is at the centre of serious religious enquiry.

Krishnamurti had asked the audience on the 9 November, 'Is there something already here for which, if it exists, one has to give one's mind and heart?' He was speaking as one who had done exactly that — 'given mind and heart' and the whole of his long life to 'preserving the sacred'. We must remind ourselves that Krishnamurti was approaching the end of that long life, and that he was addressing a group of men who had spent their lives preserving an ancient religious tradition, but in an entirely different way. For Krishnamurti that sense of preservation was not good enough. He had set his face against the whole paraphernalia of organized religion — its dogma, churches, saints, rituals, sacred books and gurus — since 1929 when he had written:

When Krishnamurti dies, which is inevitable, you will set about forming rules in your minds, because the individual, Krishnamurti, had represented to you the Truth. So you will build a temple, you will then begin to have ceremonies, to invent phrases, dogmas, systems of beliefs, creeds and to create philosophies. If you build great foundations upon me, the individual, you will be caught in that house, in that temple and so you will have to have another Teacher come and extricate you from that temple. But the human mind is such that you will build another temple round Him, and so it will go on and on.

The first two public talks at Rajghat fell on 18 and 19 November. Krishnamurti asked his audience why they were there, and then told them that he had no intention of either raising abstract, theoretical questions or helping them as a guru, but that they should think of him as a friend with whom they were talking over the problems of daily living.

During the public question and answer session someone in the audience asked how the teaching could be sustained without distortion. Krishnamurti seized on the question and said that the question whether his teaching would become corrupted or not 'depends upon you, not upon somebody else. If it means nothing except words, then it will go the way of the rest. If it means something very deep to you, to you personally, then it won't be corrupted.' Consistently and uncompromisingly, until the end, Krishnamurti put his faith in people, in their ability to hold the teaching in an understanding heart and mind.

On the 22nd, at the end of the last talk, he told his audience that they should not fall at his feet but they could come and hold his hands. And he remained sitting silently thus for a long time. For us it was like an omen, a sign that he would never come back.

When Krishnamurti came to Rishi Valley in November, we knew that he was in failing health. We hoped that Rishi Valley would revive him as it had done so often in the past, but this did not happen. On the first day we decided to walk toward the temple of the ancient goddess Gangamma which lay on the path that led past our vegetable garden and the dry bed of a monsoon stream. But he could not walk across that dry bed to the tamarind grove. Beyond that tamarind grove the valley opened out in all directions to the encircling hills turning purple at twilight. It was a sight that had often held him in awe.

After that we tried easier walks along the main road to the mouth of the valley. From one of these walks he returned very radiant and spoke of the sanctity of the place.

His daily walks became shorter as time passed and he continued to lose weight at an alarming rate. But he was happy in his room, up in the Old Guest House, surrounded by Gopalu* and Parameshwaran†, inviting people to lunch and chatting with the Hoopoe bird which he had befriended. Several times, standing outside the door of his room, we heard him say quietly to someone, 'You and your children are certainly welcome to come in here. But I assure you that you won't like it. In a few days I'll be gone, the room will be locked, the windows shut, and you will not be able to get out.'

When we entered the room, we could see the bird, framed by the picture window, sitting on the branch of the Spathodia tree, its crest fanned out, listening to Krishnamurti who lay on his bed talking in measured tones. Krishnamurti explained that the bird had become used to his voice and liked to sit and listen. Very often when small groups of us sat on the carpet in his room, the bird would swoop down, peck at the window pane and generally make a racket. And Krishnamurti would say, 'Here comes my friend,' or 'Not now, my friend.'

Another time, as we were coming into his room, we heard him say, 'So your daughter's name is Sujata. Wasn't Sujata Buddha's wife?' I thought he was chatting with the Hoopoe, but he was talking to Gopalu who had told him about the birth of a little daughter named Sujata.‡

Despite failing health Krishnamurti talked to the children and the teachers of the school. To the children he talked about fear and how important it is to be free of fear. To the teachers he talked about goodness and its connection with wholeness. When goodness is connected with wholeness it is not part of the past, of received opinion; it is not a conclusion but a discovery.

* One of the attendants at Rishi Valley
† Krishnamurti's cook at Rishi Valley
‡According to Buddhist scriptures, Sujata is the name of the low-caste girl from whom Buddha first accepted food after realizing that starvation of the body cannot lead to enlightenment.

An international conference of teachers from the various Krishnamurti schools in India and abroad had been organized to coincide with this visit. There were teachers from Brockwood Park in England and from The Oak Grove School in Ojai, California. It was the first conference of its kind, and initially Krishnamurti had seemed reluctant to participate. But once we got started he came often and unexpectedly, questioned, prodded and joked us into seriousness.

His last talk at Rishi Valley (he called it 'my last show') was an unscheduled one, prompted by questions put to him by one of the teachers. At the end of his life he continued to ask the questions he had always asked: What is goodness? What is it to flower in goodness? He also asked: What is the origin of life? What is creation?

Krishnamurti left Rishi Valley for Madras on 22 December. He rested for a few days and then gave the first of his Madras public talks on Saturday, 28 December. Clearly it was an ordeal; he was not entirely sure he would be able to go through with it. His delivery lacked some of its normal clarity, but he was exhilarated afterwards. Finding renewed energy within himself, he was eager to carry on with the scheduled question and answer session. But that session was cancelled, to preserve his strength, and an additional public talk was announced for the following Wednesday.

His temperature had risen and doctors were called. Having found no immediate cause for his fever, they recommended diagnostic tests. Krishnamurti decided to have these tests done in California under the supervision of a doctor he knew and trusted. His Bombay talks were cancelled, and the date of his return to Ojai was moved forward.

With all his dwindling energies focussed on the Madras

talks, Krishnamurti spent long hours in his room. Then he
tried to befriend a new set of hoopoe birds, this time without
success. He often chanted in solitude. As we listened from
the balcony outside his room, we were drawn into the
rhythm of his voice. He used the Sanskrit manner of
chanting, detaching the sense and concentrating completely
on the sound. But the words were from Tennyson's last
poem, 'Crossing the Bar'. Only later, reflecting on the
meaning of what we had heard, did those words begin to
signify:

> Sunset and evening star,
>  And one clear call for me!
> And may there be no moaning of the bar,
>  When I put out to sea.

> But such a tide as moving seems asleep,
>  Too full for sound and foam,
> When that which drew from out the boundless deep
>  Turns again home.

Having delivered the last of his public talks on Sunday, 4
January, Krishnamurti turned his full attention to the
destiny of the Foundations which had been set up in his
name. He understood very clearly the process whereby
religions grow when religious leaders die: deification of the
teacher; revision of his teachings, clamour for the borrowed
glory of succession. All this was a source of grave concern to
him. Having repudiated organized religion, he now met for
the last time with an organization bearing his name. What
should be done? Should the Foundations be dissolved? Was
there any way to prevent individuals from setting themselves
up as authorities on the teachings and the teacher? He
addressed these questions to the Foundation members who
were assembled there.

Some of those present were in favour of dissolving the Foundations. Others pointed out legal complications in doing so. All his life Krishnamurti had worked to set men free. Now it was our turn to set him free. For once in the course of many years, his questions were turned back upon him. The next day, in deference to Krishnamurti's wishes the following clause was appended to the Rules and Regulations of The Krishnamurti Foundation India:

Under no circumstances will the Foundation or any of the institutions under its auspices, or any of its members set themselves up as authorities on Krishnamurti's teachings. This is in accordance with Krishnamurti's declaration that no one anywhere should set himself up as an authority on him or his teaching.

Before the meetings ended Krishnamurti addressed the Foundation formally for the last time, an address which he conducted as a dialogue with Pandit Jagannath Upadhyaya.

He had very few possessions, which he proceeded to distribute — some clothes; twin cupboards which Mrs Besant had presented to him and to his brother Nitya; odds and ends; a well thumbed dictionary.

The last day was reserved for resting in preparation for the arduous flight back across the Pacific. Krishnamurti withdrew to his room and we listened as Pandit Upadhyaya retold the story of the Buddha's last moments: In the outskirts of Kuhinara the Buddha lay between two Sala trees, surrounded by disciples and a crowd of townspeople. When the end seemed near, his disciples asked the crowd to move back so the Buddha could see for one more time the open sky. At that moment when the emptiness of the sky merged with the emptiness of nirvana, the Buddha died.

Panditji, immersed in the oral traditions of Pali and Sanskrit, ended his discourse by reciting, with great tenderness, a long poem about Krishnamurti. When the recitation was over, Panditji took one of the members aside and instructed her: 'Tell him not to invite Death. Say to him these words three times: *There is still untold suffering in this world. There are people who need your help. Your work is not done.*'

She went up to Krishnamurti's room, but the words stuck in her throat and she could not speak. Seeing her difficulty, he called for his medicine to help the moment pass. He could not pour it from the bottle because the trembling of his hands had become severe. Her own hands were unsteady. Like some latter day Sujata, she had a fleeting conviction that the medicine would restore Krishnamurti's vitality if it reached him without spilling but the outcome would be disastrous if a single drop were to spill. It was another tense moment, but a luminous one; and it too passed successfully.

With some confidence restored, she conveyed Panditji's message exactly according to instructions. Krishnamurti replied that he did not want to invite Death, but he was not sure how long his body would carry on; already he had lost 13 pounds. 'Do you know what will happen if I lose any more?' he explained, 'I will not be able to walk. If that happens and I can't give any more talks then the body will die — it was meant for that purpose only.'

That day many people came to see Krishnamurti, for word had gone around that he was ill and might not return. It was tiring for him to see everyone individually, but many had come from afar to pay their respects.

In the evening he went for his last walk on the Adyar beach where he had been 'discovered' so long ago. At the end of his walk he bade a long goodbye to the four quarters, turning around full square — to the East, to the South, to the West, to the North — in that solemn farewell known as 'the elephant's turn' in ancient times.

RADHIKA HERZBERGER

# THE TALKS

# VARANASI

## DISCUSSION WITH BUDDHISTS
### 7 November 1985

*First Participant\* (P1):* So far as I have understood, you say that life has no purpose or aim and therefore there is no path to tread. Therefore each person is faced with every moment by itself. If the moment is to be understood, then the same moment is the moment of action, knowledge and desire. Is this understanding correct?

KRISHNAMURTI (K): If I may point out, we are not discussing what is correct or not correct. Sir, this is a subject that requires a great deal of inquiry.

*P1:* If you say that this is not a question of correctness or otherwise, you are creating a problem for the people who want to understand.

K: No. On the contrary, I am saying that Panditji and all of us, including myself, are going to investigate. I don't say, 'That is right, this is wrong', but together we are going to go into it.

*P1:* How can there be a human being who does not decide what is correct or incorrect, what is good or not good?

K: We will come to that. I don't say there is no goodness. Goodness may be entirely different from *your* goodness and

---

\* The chief participant in these discussions with Buddhists (P1) is Pandit Jagannath Upadhyaya.

*my* goodness. So let us find out which is really *the* good — not yours or mine, but that which is good . . .

*P2:*  . . . in itself.

K: Yes.

*P1:* You are introducing an uncertainty into one's way of looking at things or one's philosophical outlook.

K: Yes, but if you start with certainty, you end up with uncertainty.

*P1:* This also sounds very paradoxical — that you start with certainty and end up with uncertainty.

K: Of course. This is daily life. So, sir, because you raised a question which implies time, thought, action, could we begin by first going into the question of what is time? Not according to the Buddha, or to some scripture, but what is time? He will interpret it one way, the scientists will say that it is a series of small actions, thoughts and so on. Or you might say, well, time is death, time is living, or thought is time. Right? So, could we, for the time being, put aside what other people have said, including the Buddha, including what I have said or haven't said — wipe all that out — and say, 'Now, what is time?'

  Is this the only problem we have in life — time — not only a series of events, but being born, growing, dying, time as the past, future and present? We live in time. The moment we hope, it is time — I hope to be, I hope to become, I hope to become enlightened; all that implies time. Acquiring knowledge implies time, and the whole of living from birth to death is a problem of time. Right, sir? Am I making myself clear? So what is it that we call time?

*P1:* You have spoken about this many times, but I want to say that the moment which is knowledge, action, as well as desire, is a moment in which there is no time.

K: Wait, wait. Can you divide this instant from the rest?

*P1:* In the instant of attention or observation, there is no time.

K: What do you mean, observation and attention? Sorry to be so analytical. But if we are to understand each other we must be clear about the meaning of these two words — attention and observation. What takes place actually when you observe? — not theoretically. When you observe that tree, that bird, that woman, that man, what takes place?

*P2:* In that moment of observation, if it is real observation . . .

K: Is it? I am asking. When he uses the word observation, what does he mean by that? I may mean one thing, he may mean another, she may mean yet another thing.

*P2:* But you are asking Panditji what *he* means by observation.

K: And what he means by attention . . . Sir, may I ask a question? Could we start to discuss, to have a dialogue, a conversation on a word, which is really very, very good deliberation? You know the meaning of that word deliberate? The word comes from *libra* which in Greek means balance, weigh. You have the same thing in the Zodiac — Libra. And from *libra* comes the word liberate. And also it comes from the word *deliberare* which in Italian means 'to sit down, talk over, take counsel with each other, weigh together'. It is not you offering an opinion and I offering another opinion, but both of us taking counsel together, both of us weighing because we want to find the truth of it. Not I will find it and then tell you — that does not exist in that word deliberate. Sir, when the Pope is elected in Rome, in the Sistine Chapel in the Vatican, they deliberate — the doors are locked, nobody can get out, they have their own places for toilet, restaurant, food; everything is arranged for a fortnight or for some days. Within those set days they must settle. That is called deliberation. So could we start, both of us, as though we know nothing?

*P3:* It is difficult for Panditji.

K: It is not difficult. I know nothing; our knowledge is merely memory. What's the point of it? I am saying, knowledge may be the greatest danger in the world; it may be the greatest hindrance. To further knowledge we are adding, the scientists are adding. That which is added to is always limited.

*P2:* Of course. If it is complete, you cannot add to it.

K: Yes. Therefore your knowledge is always limited, and if you discuss from that limitation, you end up in limitation.

*P2:* And the so-called certainty is that limitation.

K: Yes, limitation.

*P1:* We have heard quite a bit from you and understood certain things; but if the understanding has to be at a deeper level, then someone like you has the responsibility of making that known, since we are at different levels.

K: All right, all right. But the man says, K says, leave your moorings, let us float together.

*P1:* How can we counsel together when we are at two different levels?

K: I don't admit that. I don't admit that we are at two levels.

*P1:* We have a complaint against you that . . .

K: . . .that I am a poor surgeon!

*P1:* . . .physician, yes. Because there are all the difficulties and conflicts outside. People like me who have the privilege of coming to you receive some light, but the physician is not able to say how to cope with those things which are outside and solve the difficulties there.

K: So you want to solve first the difficulties out there, and then approach the problems in here. Is that it?

*P1:* No, I want to solve them both together.

K: I do not admit the division.

*P1:* Yes, I accept that.

K: The world is me, I am the world. Now, from there how do we solve the problem?

*P1:* Let us say I don't make a difference between outer and inner things.

K: First make sure of that. Do you actually see that, or is it theoretical?

*P1:* For me it is theoretical.

K: Sir, first of all, theory to me has no value. Forgive me, sir. I see what is happening in the world — war, nationalities, killing, all the appalling things that are happening — *actually* happening. I am not imagining it; I see it happening under my nose. Now, who created it?

*P1:* Human beings.

K: Do you admit that we all of us have created that?

*P2:* Yes, of course.

K: All right. So, if all of us have created it, then we can change that. Now, in what manner will you bring about the change? Sir, I met the other day in New York, a scientist, a doctor who has become a philosopher. He said this is all talk, the real question is: can the cells in the brain bring about a mutation in themselves — not through drugs, not through various genetic processes, but can the brain cells themselves say: This is wrong — change! Do you understand, sir? Can the brain cells themselves, uninfluenced, undrugged, see what they have created and say: This is wrong — mutate!

*P1:* But you distinguish the brain from the mind.

K: Yes, may be silly, but I have made a difference because the brain is the very centre of our sensations.

*P4:* Sir, that was my question the day before yesterday also: Should we wait for that mutation?

K: You can't. It will go on.

*P4:* Will it come automatically?

K: No

*P4:* So we should try for that.

K: What will you do, sir? You see that a mutation is necessary. Right?

*P4:* Yes, everyone agrees with that.

K: Now, what will change that? — in the cells, not just ideas. The very cells of the brain contain all the memories of the past. Can those cells, without pressure, without influence, without chemicals, say: That is the end of that; I will change?

*P2:* No. If there is no influence, no pressure, it means it is taking place by itself.

K: No. Listen to it. The brain cells hold all the memories, all the pressures, all the education, all the experience, everything — it is the centre of knowledge. Right?

*P2:* Yes, it is loaded.

K: Loaded with knowledge of two and a half million years. We have tried everything — chemicals, torture, every form of experience to bring about a change inside the skull; we have not succeeded. There is genetic engineering, there is every form of experiment being done to change this inside, but they haven't succeeded. They haven't so far; they may in a thousand years. So I say to myself, why does this brain depend on all this — chemicals, persuasion, pleasure? Is it waiting to be released? I say, 'No, sorry, that is another form of escape.'

*P2:* Waiting for something else.

K: Yes. So, can the brain cells, with all the past memories, put an end to all that now? That is my question. What do you say, sir?

*P1:* I have another question. I have to teach my students and I do it through a logical process — rationally so many things are explained. At the same time I realize the limitation of that, especially having come into contact with you — that this is all artificial, theoretical, very limited. Then, when we come to you, we hear what is good, and we go from one fine point to another, but I find at the end of it all that we are still nowhere near the truth. So it just means that instead of going round in that circle of logic we go round in this, but it makes no difference.

K: Yes, sir, these are all just explanations and we move from that logic to this logic. So, do we see that logic has a limitation? Now, can I leave that logic without going to another logic, because I see at the very beginning that logic has limitation — whether it is superfine logic or plain common sense?

*P1:* No, the two cannot be compared because the other is entirely logical, which we understand is limited, but here it is not just logic as we get bits of insight, bits of light; but we keep moving around with these little bits. There is no comprehension.

K: All right. If that is so — which I question — is it that you want complete insight? Your question implies that.

*P1:* We should be satisfied with what we are getting, but we need that happiness which shapes thought. We get little bits of insight, not the whole.

K: I am not talking of happiness; I am talking of insight. Will you listen to it? I will present the whole, I will show you logically the whole. Will you listen — not say yes, this is right, this is wrong? Sir, practically every writer, painter, scientist, poet, guru — they all have a limited insight. You and I come along and say, 'Look, this is limited, and I want the real, complete, full insight; not partial.' Right?

*P1:* We need to understand this. What is full insight? Is it an experience?

K: No, I doubt if it is an experience. It is not an experience.

*P2:* Then it has to come from within.

K: No, you see, you are already stipulating what should happen.

*P2:* It cannot be anticipated.

K: You cannot lay down laws about it. You cannot say it is experience; it is not.

*P2:* You were going to tell us how all this will be a whole.

K: Not all this; the parts do not make the whole. I am as damned logical as any of you. I am just saying, you are approaching it wrongly. That is my point; don't say it is an experience; it is based on knowledge. What is based on knowledge is invention, not creation.

*P6:* Sir, he is not saying it is experience based on knowledge, but it has to be real, proved.

K: It is not that I experience something; it is real. I don't understand your difficulty. Somebody comes along and tells me a story. I listen with rapt attention. It is a beautiful story, lovely language, style; I am enraptured by it, I listen to the story, and it goes on and on day after day, and I am consumed by the story. So the story ends by saying, 'It stops here.'

*P5:* The story doesn't end for us; the problem continues.

K: You are my friend. I want to tell you that people have limited insight, which is obvious. Your friend here says, I will tell you in what manner you can have the whole insight. Will you listen to him? Don't argue, just listen. You give rice to the beggar; he didn't expect anything from you, but you give it. In the same way, he is giving me a gift and he says, 'Take it, don't ask me why you are being given it, who is giving it; just take it.' So I am telling you, insight is not dependent on the intellect, it is not dependent on knowledge, it is not dependent on any form of remembrance, and it is not dependent on time. Enlightenment is not dependent on time. Time, memory, remembrance, cause — they don't exist; then you have insight, complete insight. Sir, like two ships passing each other at night, one says to the other, 'This is it,' and passes on. What will you do?

*P4:* Sir, does it come through gradual practice or is it instantaneous?

K: Practice means memory, time.

*P4:* So it can only be instantaneous.

K: Oh no, no, sir, just listen. He tells me this and he disappears. He has left with me a tremendous jewel and I am watching the beauty of it. I am not saying, why did he give it to me, who is he, and so on. He has given it to me and he said, 'Take it, my friend, live with it, and if you don't want it, throw it away.' And I never see him again. I am enthralled by the jewel, and that jewel begins to reveal things I have never seen before, and that jewel says, 'Hold me more closely, you will see much more.' But I say, 'I have got my wife, my children, my college, my university, my job; I can't do this.' So you put it on the table, come back in the evening, and you look at it. But the jewel is fading, so you have to hold it, you have to cherish it, love it, watch it, care for it.

I am not trying to convince anybody of anything. We see that our knowledge is very limited, and knowledge may be the very danger, it may be the poison in all of us.

Sir, I met the other day, just before I came to India, three computer experts — the very, very latest. They are going deeper into artificial intelligence. And artificial intelligence can do most of the things that human beings can do — argue, have tremendous knowledge, much more than any of us. It will include British knowledge, European knowledge, French knowledge, Russian knowledge, all the Upanishads, all the Gitas, all the Bibles, the Korans, everything, and it will act — it will tell you what to eat, what not to eat, when to go to bed for your health, when you cannot have sex, everything you can do; it has already begun. And what is going to happen to the human brain if that machine can do everything I can do, except have sex or look at the stars? What is the point of the human being? And the entertainment industry — football, tennis, all these things — here too, unfortunately, it is very strong. So if man is caught in all the entertainment, which includes all the religious entertainment, then where is man? Sir, this is a very serious question; it is not just casual talk.

*P2:* This question would not arise if there is mutation in the brain which is then far ahead of the present brain, because the present brain is memory and the machine has a far better memory.

K: A little chip like that holds 600 million words.

*P2:* All the libraries of the world will be in the machine.

K: They have got it, haven't they? Therefore, why should I go to the library, why should I listen to all this stuff? Therefore, entertainment.

*P2:* Or mutate.

K: That's it. This is the question I have been asking.

*P2:* So we are back to the question.

*P1:* Does meditation have a place in all this?

K: Yes. Sir, is there a meditation which is not contrived, which is not deliberate, which does not say practise, practise, practise, which had nothing to do with all this? Because, that way I practise to become a rich man, I have a deliberate purpose. So it can't be meditation as we do it now. So, perhaps there is a meditation which has nothing to do with all this — and I say there is.

*P2:* Shall we stop here?

K: Yes, we stop — like the story.

# VARANASI

Krishnamurti (K): Is there something sacred, something long-lasting, and not conditioned by commerce? Is there something in India, in this part of the world?

*First Participant (P1):* There is certainly something in this country which is not influenced by external factors.

K: That was not my question. Is there something here which does not exist anywhere else — not influenced, not corrupted, not made ugly by all the circus that goes on in the name of religion? Is there something already here, for which — if it exists — one has to give one's whole mind and heart — to preserve? You understand, sir?

*P1:* I cannot say, because in some sense I have not experienced this in a tangible way; nor can I say whether other people have. But my study of ancient texts gives me a certain certitude that there is something which can be experienced in a clear way.

K: I'm asking, Panditji, if there is something enduring, which is not bound by time, evolution and all that. It must be very, very sacred. And if it exists, then one must give one's life to it, protect it, give vitality to it — not by doctrines and knowledge, but by the feeling of it, the depth of it, the beauty of it, the enormous strength of it. That's what I'm asking.

*P1:* We desire to find such a thing, but have not been able to do so. And our experience is such that we find ourselves tangled in many theories, in many traditions, many systems. Occasionally we hear a clear voice that speaks about this in a compelling way. That voice comes from you, but we are in some way unable to reach it. The whole phenomenon is like some huge fair with a lot of different chaotic voices offering solutions.

K: You're not answering my question: is there or is there not? Not tradition, not a kind of historical process of ancient culture diminishing, being destroyed by commercialism, but the great impetus which was set going by some power, some intelligence? That power, that intelligence — does it exist now? I'm repeating the same thing in different words.

P2: If I have to answer your question, then I would say that what you're talking about — that thing — is life.

K: I'm asking a very simple question; don't complicate it. India exploded over the whole of Asia, like Greece exploded over the whole of Western culture. I'm not talking about India geographically, but as part of the world. It spread like wildfire. And it had the tremendous energy of something original, something enormous; it had the power to move things. Does that exist here, or is it all in abeyance? Does it exist at all now?

P3: I don't know, sir. I think it exists.

K: Why? Why do you think that?

P3: Sometimes it appears, but not usually.

K: It's like a breath of fresh air. If that air is constantly flowing, it's always fresh.

P3: It is always flowing, it is always fresh, but the contact with persons is not always there.

K: I understand that, but it's not good enough.

*P2:* Why do you want to connect it geographically with this part of the world?

K: Geographically — I'll tell you. All ancients, as far as I understand, worshipped mountains. The gods came from there for the Greeks; and for the ancient Sumerians, again the mountains, the sense of something holy there. Then you come to the Himalayas — it's all in the *Dakshinamurti Stotra.* The monks lived there, meditated there. Is it there still, or is it being commercialized?

*P3:* It is there, it cannot be commercialized. The commercialization is something else.

K: Is it there?

*P3:* Yes.

K: Why do you say yes?

*P3:* Because it is there. It is . . .

K: Sir, you are there, physically. I can theorize how the body is constructed, but you are still there — to touch, to feel, to see, to actually see you are sitting there. Is there such a thing?

*P3:* Yes, it is there, actually there. It is there.

K: It is no good telling me, 'It is there, it is there.' If it is there, why has this part of the world been so corrupt, so appalling? You don't realize what I'm saying.

*P3:* From the beginning I am saying that it is there, but the relationship, the contact, with the masses . . .

K: I'm not talking about the masses. It's you, you . . .

*P3:* With the persons . . .

K: With you . . .

*P3:* It is diminished.

K: Why has it decreased, why has it diminished, why has it become something small?

*P3:* People are not interested.

K: So what does that mean?

*P3:* They're more interested in commerce.

K: Yes. So it's gone. That doesn't matter. Let's leave that question. Or is it this tremendous self-interest — self-interest in the form of knowledge, in the form of Buddhism, Hinduism? It is all basically self-interest. And that self-interest is increasing tremendously in the world, and that is the door which shuts the other out. You understand?

Sir, some time ago three very clever people — they were scientists — came to Brockwood, and we were talking. They are trying to find artificial intelligence. If they can find that, then we are all gone. Your knowledge, your Vedas, your Upanishads and your Geeta — everything is gone, because the machine can repeat it much better than you and I can ever do.

*P1:* The question which you just posed presents a wonderful opportunity to ask a counter question. And the counter question is: What you say appeals to us, but how are we, in today's society, going to find it, experience it, and share it?

K: You can't experience it. To experience it there must be an experiencer. He has had a thousand experiences; he adds another to it — that's my whole point. It's not an experience; it's not something that I and you experience. It's there like electricity. I can admire it, worship it, but it's there.

*P1:* Human beings have only one gift, that is the ability to experience, and you are snatching that away. After that what are we to hold on to?

K: I'm not snatching anything away, but I see that experience is a very small affair. I experience; then what?

Experience gives you knowledge of how to climb a mountain. We depend on experience, but *that* thing can't be experienced. You can't *experience* water; it is there. I can experience sex; I can experience something hitting me; I can experience somebody praising me.

*P4:* Water is there, but I only know it through experience of it.

K: You only know because you perceive it. You know the quality of it; you float on it; but all that is part of your knowledge of it.

*P2:* But if I had no knowledge, I wouldn't have any experience.

K: What you call experience is based on sensory perception. And our sensory perceptions are partial, never complete. Now, to observe with all your senses alert — that's not an experience. Sir, I look at that piece of cloth and say it's red, because I've been conditioned to call it red. If you'd been conditioned to call it purple, you'd call it purple. The brain is always conditioned by our experience, by our sensory responses — how to argue, how to deny and all the rest of it.

If I happen to be a Catholic my whole attitude towards religion is Jesus, Virgin Mary and all the rest of it. You are a Hindu or Buddhist — sorry, I'm not comparing — and everything is from that conditioning. Therefore, when you say experience, or you must learn this or do that, it's all from a brain which has become small, conditioned.

*P3:* We again come to that point we discussed. We understand about conditioning, self-interest, and so on. There is the possibility of moving away, and then we just stop there.

K: Why, sir?

*P3:* Or should I say that the moving away is not absolutely possible?

K: Or remain where you are — you understand? — and not move away. Remain where you are and see what happens. That is, sir, you never stay whole, abide with *what* is.

*P3:* Yes, that is obvious.

K: Wait, sir, wait, wait. We never stay there. We're always moving, moving. Right? I am this, I will be that — it's a movement away from *what is.*

*P3:* Either we stay where it is, or stay out of the movement.

K: What is the movement?

*P3:* Change, force . . .

K: Then we have to understand what is time, the movement in time.

*P3:* Yes.

K: We have to enquire what is time — that which we live daily: time as past, time as present, time as future. So what is time? You understand, sir? It requires a lot of time to learn Sanskrit, to enquire into the earliest doctrines, various literatures — what the ancients said, what the Buddha said, what Nagarjuna said, and so on. To learn a skill requires time, to cover a distance from here to there requires time. Everything we do requires time. Then we must inquire: What is time?

*P4:* Time is the means of achieving.

K: Yes, success, failure, acquiring a skill, learning a language, writing a letter, covering a distance from here to there and so on. To us that is time. What is time?

*P4:* It's a movement in the mind, a subtle, incessant movement of the mind.

K: Then what is the brain? What is the mind? Don't invent. Look at it. What is the brain?

*P5:* It's very difficult to make out the difference between the brain and the mind. The involuntary, almost incessant way of thoughts pouring into unknown stimuli, is what accounts for time.

K: No, sir, you are not listening. There's time by the clock: to cover a distance, to learn a language, it requires time. And also we have lived on this earth for two and a half million years. There's been a tremendous evolution, which is time. What do you mean by time?

*P4:* All that you've just mentioned is physical time. But the real problem of time seems to hinge on how it works within the psyche. There is something unresolved that we want to resolve.

K: Sir, before we talk of the mind, if I may humbly suggest, what is the brain?

*P4:* The brain is possibly the physical base or biological structure of the mind.

K: The brain is the centre of all our action, centre of all our sensory responses; it is the centre of all thinking, inside the skull. What is the quality of the brain that is asking the question: what is time? How do you receive the question?

*P1:* We have understood after discussing with you that it is only total attention that will bring about a total transformation. That's where the problem begins.

K: Would you mind if I say something? Time is the past, time is now; and the now is controlled by the past, shaped by the past. And the future is a modification of the present. I'm putting it dreadfully simply. So the future is *now*. Therefore the question is: If all time is contained in the now, all time — past, present and future — then what do we mean by change?

*P1:* The word 'change' does not have any meaning.

K: No, wait. The now contains all time. If that's a fact — a *fact*, not a theory, not some kind of speculative conclusion — that all time is contained in the now, this is the future, this is the present. There is no movement towards or for. There is *no* movement. Movement implies time, right? So there is *no* change. Change becomes idiotic. Then I am what I am: I am greedy, and I say yes.

*PI:* There is a wide difference between you and us; we may be saying the same thing.

K: Oh, no, no. I don't admit anything of the kind.

*PI:* You are saying that all time is now. I also say the same thing: All time is now. But my saying and your saying are two totally different things.

K: Why?

*P4:* Because he says it from logic and speculation.

K: That's it. That means time is operating.

*PI:* How can we remove this difficulty?

*P4:* Panditji, answer the question: How can we break this stream in which we flow?

*PI:* The stream is broken through logic. There is a big gulf between you and us. I understand what you're saying speculatively. The problem is: How do we remove this gulf? Because, we have reached a certain meeting, in the sense of understanding.

K: I'll tell you. No, I'll show you. Please, I'm not a guru. Is this a fact? — time is now; all time is contained in now, at this second. Really, this is a most extraordinary thing: to see that the future, the past, is now. Is that a fact — not an idea of the fact?

*P4:* There are two things: perceiving and conceiving. Now I am conceiving, not perceiving.

K: So what's the point of it?

*P4:* No point, but I would like to go on from here — from conception to perception.

K: Conception is not a fact.

*P4:* Conception is not a fact; perception is a fact, and we are all caught up in conception, in time. The simultaneity of conception and time has to be broken. One has to get away from . . .

K: Who gets away?

*P4:* I mean, for perception to operate.

K: The very word 'operation' means time.

*P6:* Just a minute. If I may come in at this point and say one thing: If all time is in the now, then there is nothing else.

K: Which means what?

*P6:* That you stop looking.

K: Now you're already preconceiving.

*P6:* I'm not preconceiving. If all time is now . . .

K: That may be the most extraordinary thing, if you go into it. That may be the essence of compassion. That may be the essence of amazing, undefinable intelligence. You can't say all time is now if it isn't a reality. The other things don't matter. I don't know if I am making myself clear.

Sir, if all time is contained in the now, there's no movement. What I do now, I'll do tomorrow. So tomorrow is now. What am I to do if the future — tomorrow — is now? I'm greedy, envious, and I'll be envious tomorrow. Is there a possibility of ending that greed *instantly?*

*P1:* That is very difficult.

K: It's not difficult at all. I see that if I am greedy today, envious today, tomorrow I'll be greedy and envious unless something happens now. It is very important that something happen *now*. So can I change, mutate, *now*?

There is a movement which is not of time if there is a radical mutation. You understand, sir? Two and a half million years ago we were barbarous. We are still barbarous; wanting power, position, killing each other, envious, comparing, all that. You've put me this challenge: All time is *now*. I have no escape points, I've no gates through which I can escape from this central fact. I say to myself: My god, if I don't change now, tomorrow will be the same, or a thousand tomorrows. So, is it possible for me to totally mutate *now*? I say yes.

*P4:* Can you tell us how?

K: Not *how*, sir. The moment you say *how*, you are already in the process of time: I tell you this, this, this, and you say I will do this, this to get to that. You can't get it because *you are what you are now.*

*P6:* That means that in the listening to that statement of yours, 'All time is now', there is a quality of acquisitiveness.

K: Of course.

*P6:* So the listening has to be purified.

K: So, sir, there is no knowledge, there is no meditation, there is no discipline. Everything stops. May I put the question differently? Suppose for instance I know I'm going to die. There is a time interval between now and death: that is, I will die on the first of January. (I'm not actually going to die on the first of January!) Doctors have told me say, that I have terminal cancer and I can't survive the first of January. So I've got a couple of months to die. If all time is now, I am dying. So I don't have time; I don't want time. So death is now. Can the human brain live with death all the time? You understand?

I'm going to die — that's certain. And I say, For god's sake wait a minute. But if I realize the fact that all time is now — that means death and living are together; they are never separate. So knowledge is dividing me — knowledge that I'm going to die at the end of January — and I get frightened; I say, Please, please, wait, wait, wait, I've got to leave a will, I've got to do this, I've to do that. But if I live with death, I'm doing it all the time; that is, I draw up my will. I'm dying now, that means I'm living. I'm living and death is next door; there's no divorce or separation between living and dying.

Can you do this, sir, or is it impossible? That means death says, 'You can't take anything with you.' Your knowledge, your books, your wife and children, your money, your character, your vanity, all that you've built up for yourself — everything goes at the end with death. You may say there's a possibility you'll reincarnate. But I'm asking you: Can you live now without the least attachment to anything? Why postpone this — which is attachment — until the sickbed? Be free of attachment *now*.

*P6:* May we sit silently with you?

(K *assents*)

*P1:* You had started the discussion with the question: What is this thing, and, is there this thing in this country? Is *this* that thing?

K: (*nods, then after a long silence*) See, it's not difficult. It's so simple. I don't want personally any reputation; I don't want a sense of 'I know and you don't know.' By nature I'm a very humble man, very shy, respectful, gentle. So what do you want? You understand, sir? If you can start at that level . . . Right. That's enough. Let me tell you a joke.

There were three holy men in the Himalayas — of course, it has to be the Himalayas! Ten years pass, one of them says:

'Oh, what a lovely evening this is!' Another ten years pass and the other man says, 'I hope it will rain.' Another ten years pass and the third man says: 'I wish you two would be quiet.'

# VARANASI

KRISHNAMURTI (K): Sir, I would like to ask several questions. Is there a line, a demarcation, where self-interest ends and where a state which is not self-interest begins? We all have self-interest; it is in knowledge, in language, in science, in every part of our life. In every way of our life there is self-interest, and that has created havoc. And how far does it extend? And where do we draw the line and say: here it is necessary, there it is not necessary at all? — in daily life; not in science, in mathematics, in knowledge. I am talking factually, not theoretically.

*First Participant (P1):* This question is very difficult to answer if you lay down certain conditions, like the difficulties we meet with in society; but if you do not lay down conditions, then I shall try to answer.

K: All right, I remove the conditions. Not remove; life is this. I am not laying down the condition, I am not laying down the law, the way you should think, but life shows me that in every work in every part of the world self-interest is dominant. We play with religion, we play with K as a plaything, we play with all kinds of things, but the thread of self-interest is very, very strong, and I ask myself, where does it begin, and, is there an end to it. Where does it start, where does it end, or is there no end at all? God is my self-interest, so are ceremonies, scholarship, science. The man in the corner who sells tobacco there, is full of self-interest.

*P₁:* There is some book-learning that underlies my answer, but I will try to answer from my experiences as an individual human being.

K: Yes, as a human being — even from your books, from your studies, you must have, they must all have, asked this question in different ways.

*P₁:* When I try to understand myself, look at myself as I am, factually, then I put myself into certain categories. When I try to discover myself in action, in my relationship to other people, then I find an element of self-interest, and I can, with some effort, try to be free of this self-interest, and I do unburden myself to a certain extent.

K: But that is also self-interest.

*P₁:* When I try to establish my existence, my being, then my actions become more self-centred, and to the extent to which I unburden myself, the self-interest decreases.

K: No, you are missing my point. I want to make it very, very simple. The more simply we think, the better the action, the better the way of looking at things. From childhood the problems begin — I have to go to school, I have to read and learn, I have to learn mathematics. The whole of life becomes a problem because, basically, I meet life as a problem. In the English language a problem means something thrown at you. *Problema* comes from Greek; it means something hurled at you and you have to reply to it. So, from childhood, my brain is conditioned to live with problems and solve problems — and those problems can never be solved. I keep this going, problem after problem; all my life becomes a problem, living becomes a problem. And I say, I don't want to live that way, it is wrong to live that way. So I am asking myself, does self-interest create the problem, or can the mind, brain, be free of problems and therefore tackle problems? You see the difference? I don't know if I am making myself clear. It is a fact that I have to go to school, learn, read, and so on. My brain gradually gets conditioned to living with problems, the brain becomes the problem — everything becomes a problem. So I come to you to solve the problem the brain has, which may be linked with self-interest.

*P1:* Creating or receiving problems and trying to solve them has become a rule of life for us, and this way of doing things nurtures my being.

K: Therefore your being is a problem. But you are missing my point. Your being is the identity with the country, with the literature, with the language, with the gods; you are identified, therefore you have taken root in a place, therefore that becomes the being. There is no separate being apart from that — no spiritual being, god-being — I don't believe in all that; I am entirely sceptical. So I say to myself, why have I, or you, made life, which is meant to be lived like a tree growing beautifully, into this? I can't live that way, I *won't* live that way. Whether god exists, etc. — I am totally indifferent to all that, I totally discard all that, and I say to myself, I won't live the way you are living; I won't. I will go away to the mountains rather than live that way. You have destroyed living, you have destroyed living by knowledge, by science, by computers — you have destroyed my living. I can retire into the mountains, but that makes no meaning.

*P1:* Why are you so keen to safeguard what you call living? Suppose I betray it, I break it, what difference does it make?

K: I am not saying I want to live; that is not my point. I say, why do I live this way? I am not safeguarding it by asking this. Why have I to go through all this appalling process? Sex becomes a problem, eating becomes a problem, everything is a problem. And I don't want to have problems, which does not mean that I deny life. I don't want problems, therefore I meet problems. Because my brain won't work in problems, I can meet all problems.

*P1:* As I understand it, you are saying that problems should not enter, problems should not constrain your being. You don't want to deny life, but you want not to be affected by problems.

K: No, no. You have thoroughly misunderstood me. I am saying, from birth to death life is treated like a problem: school, college, university, then job, marriage, sex, children — one of them is naughty or a genius and I utilize or exploit that boy and keep going all my life. Death then becomes a problem. Then I say, is there a living further, reincarnation and all that? You see what humanity has done? This is life. Why can't my brain be simple enough, free enough to say this is a problem and solve it? That is, the brain is free to solve it, not add another problem to it.

*P2:* If I may say so, sir, the problem does not come from outside; the problem arises in this brain, which feeds on this problem, which creates this problem. Why doesn't it immediately destroy it at that very instant?

K: Because it has not solved any problem.

*P1:* Does the brain have that capacity of ending?

K: Yes, but I must distinguish, make clear one point. The brain is the centre of all our nerves, all our sensations, all our reactions, our knowledge, our relationships, quarrels and all that. It is the centre of our consciousness, and that consciousness we treat as mine — *my* consciousness. I say, it is not mine; it is not personalized as K. And it is not yours because every human being on earth goes through this torture — pain, sorrow, pleasure, sex, fear, anxiety, uncertainty, hoping for something better and so on; that is our consciousness. So that consciousness is not yours; it is human. It is humanity. I am humanity — not all of you plus me. I am humanity.

*P3:* It seems to me that we know of two kinds of action: one which is thought out by the brain, calculated, and which therefore invariably contains the seed of self-interest, is motivated by self-interest. I don't think the brain is capable of doing anything that does not contain in it the seed of self-interest, because it is the instrument meant for that purpose. But there is also spontaneous action which we experience occasionally, which is born just out of love, not as a product of thinking. And because man does not know what to do with this kind of action, because there is nothing he can do about that kind of action, he has cultivated the other — he has cultivated what his brain can do well, what it can calculate, what it can achieve, and the whole world is therefore filled with such activity, such action. And that has become our life. And the other, which is the vital, is occasional.

K: I am not coming to that for the moment. The mind is different from the brain — totally dissociated — has no relationship whatsoever. Love has no relationship with self-interest. Don't bring in love for the moment. The fact is that love may exist. We may have sympathy, empathy, affection, pity — but that is not love, so I leave that aside. That's all for the moment. Love and self-interest cannot exist together. Problems and love cannot exist together. Therefore problems have no meaning if the other exists. If the other is, problems are not.

*P3:* I am not sure if they cannot co-exist. They are independent; but I think even a person who has self-interest and who has problems, occasionally acts without the interference of the brain — out of love. So I would not say that the existence of the brain denies love completely.

K: Sir, I say it is like having occasionally a bad egg. I want a good egg every day — not occasionally. So I am asking you all, where does self-interest begin and where does it end? Is there an end to self-interest? Or is all action born out of self-interest? Don't tell me, 'occasionally'; I am not interested in that. Occasionally I look out of the window and that window is very narrow; I am in a prison.

So please follow me for a minute. There is a tremendous order in the universe. A black hole is a part of that order. Wherever man enters he creates disorder. So I say, can I, as a human being who is the rest of humanity, create order in myself first? Order means no self-interest.

*P4:* Sir, the problem is, it is not easy to deny on the basis of a common consciousness the nucleus that comes to shape itself as the limited self, the acquisitive self, for which all the problems are real, not imaginary. I mean I have disease, I have death — in what way could these be considered as no problems?

K: Are you saying that the self is the problem? Why do we make it a problem? Why do you say the self is the problem? Perhaps we make it into a problem and then say, how am I to get out of it? We don't look at the problem. We don't say, the self is the problem, let me understand it, let me look at this jewel without condemning it. The very condemnation is the problem. Do you follow what I mean? Therefore, I won't condemn it, I won't suppress it, I won't deny it, I won't transcend it; but let me first look at it.

*P4:* Sir, consider a person who has a thorn in his body and is feeling pain. The pain of the thorn is similar to the constraints and problems impinging upon the self.

K: No, sir. If I have a thorn in my foot, I look at it first, I know the pain. I ask myself, why did I tread on it, why wasn't I aware of it? What is wrong with my observation, my eyes? Why didn't I see where I was going? I know if I saw it, I wouldn't touch it. Therefore I didn't see it. When the pain is there, then I act. I didn't see the thing that was in front of my foot. So my observation is at fault. So I say, what happened to my brain which didn't see that? Probably it was thinking of something else. Why was it thinking of something else when I am on the path? So you see, sir?

*P5:* But in the case of psychological problems, the observer and what is observed are hopelessly entangled.

K: No. We are going off to something else. Let us stick to one problem, one issue. Where does self-interest begin and where does it end, and is there an ending to it at all? And if it ends, what is that state?

*P6:* May I hazard an answer? Probably, self-interest begins with the self itself and the self comes with the body.

K: I am not sure.

*P6:* They go together. The idea of 'I'-ness and my coming into being, they go together.

K: You say so, but I don't say so.

*P6:* To my mind the very notion of self begins with the coming into being of this body, and the self and self-interest go together. Self-interest can only end when the self ends. And a part of the self remains so long as the body remains. So, in an ultimate sense, it can only end with death. Short of that, we can only refine self-interest with the gradual perceiving of it, but we cannot wholly deny it so long as the body exists. That is how I see it.

K: I understand. They are discovering in science that when the baby is born and suckling, it feels secure and it begins to learn who are the friends of the mother, who treat her differently, who are against her; it begins to feel all this because the mother feels it. It comes through the mother —

who is friendly, who is not friendly. The baby begins to rely on the mother. So there it begins. It felt very safe in the womb, and suddenly, put out in the world it begins to realize that the mother is the only safety. There it begins to be secure. And that's our life. And I question whether there is security at all.

*P2:* Sir, in the Mexican earthquake, babies were found alive eleven days after being buried completely under the earth and there was no damage to the new-born ones. And the Mexican ambassador was telling me, the child, when it was taken out of that dark place, behaved exactly as it does when it comes out of the womb.

K: It was like being still in the womb.

*P3:* Sir, the instinct of self-preservation is there in the animal too, but when it evolved into man, he started creating problems. The animal does not create problems. If we believe what the scientists say, that man evolved from the animal, then he has all the instincts which the animal has. The essential difference is that man has in addition the ability to think, and this ability to think has also created all those problems. And what you are asking is, can we use this ability not to create problems but to do something entirely different?

K: Yes, sir that's right.

*P7:* The brain is the source of all problems. It has created the self and also all the problems. You suggest that the brain can end the problems. Then what is the difference between that brain which has ended and the mind?

*P6:* You said that the brain is the source of problems and out of the brain comes the ending of problems. With that ending, the brain that remains thinks, perceives, receives intimations. What is the actual difference between that brain and the mind?

K: I understand, I understand. Just a minute. See, you are asking a question that involves death. Before I can answer that question I must answer what death is. There is an Italian proverb that says: All the world is going to die, perhaps even I too! Do you see the joke of it? So, what is death? We know what is birth — mother, father, all the rest of it, and the baby is born and goes through this extraordinary tragedy. It is a tragedy; it is not something happy, joyous, free. It is a bigger tragedy than any Shakespeare ever wrote. So I know what is birth. Now, what is death? I am asking this; you tell me.

Pɪ: When we were discussing time the other day, you spoke of a 'now' in which was all time, both living and death. The brain, having the capacity to see the flow of living, also has the capacity to reveal that ending which is death. That is the answer.

K: I said, living is attachment, pain, fear, pleasure, anxiety, uncertainty, the whole bag, and death is out there, far away. I keep a careful distance. I have got property, books, jewels; that is my life. I keep it here and death is there. I say, bring the two together, not tomorrow, but *now* — which means end all this *now*. Because that's what death is going to say. Death says you can't take anything with you; so invite death — not suicide — invite death and live with it. Death is now, not tomorrow.

Pɪ: There is something lacking in this. I may be able to invite death now and the brain may be still for a time, but the whole thing comes back again; then the problem of life comes back.

K: No, no. I am attached to him, he is a friend of mine, I have lived with him, we walked together, we played together, he is my companion, and I am attached to him. Death says to me, You can't take him with you. So death tells me, Free yourself now, not ten years later. And I say, Quite right, I will be free of him. Though I am still his friend, I am not dependent on him at all. Because, I can't take him with me. What's wrong with that? You are not arguing against that?

*P5:* Which means, sir, you have to end all gratification . . .

K: No, I am not saying that. I said, attachment.

*P5:* All attachment . . .

K: That's all.

*P8:* Sir, is it possible to end that so long as the two bodies exist?

K: Oh, yes, sir. Our bodies are not tied together; they are two separate bodies. Psychologically I take him as a friend and get slowly attached to him inwardly. I am not attached to him outwardly because he goes one way and I go another — he drinks, I don't, and so on. But still he is a friend of mine. And death comes and says you can't take him with you. That is a fact. So I say, All right, I will be detached now.

*P3:* Sir, isn't it that the problem comes not because you get pleasure from your friend or your wife, but because you begin to use that pleasure as a fulfilment for yourself, and therefore you want a continuity of that and you want to possess that person?

K: Yes. Therefore, what is relationship? I won't go into it, we have no time. You see, sir, you are not meeting my point. I asked you where self-interest begins and ends. Is ending more important than anything else? — ending? And what is then that state in which there is no self-interest at all? Is it death? — which means an ending. Death means ending — ending everything. So it says, 'Be intelligent, old boy, live together with death.'

*P3:* Which means die but keep the body. The other death is coming anyway.

K: Body? Give it to the birds or throw it into the river. But psychologically, this tremendous structure I have built I can't take with me.

*P3:* Is it an instinct, sir? Is it an inheritance through the genes?

K: Yes, probably. But animals don't think this way; I have watched several animals.

*P3:* No, therefore I am not sure if it is an instinct.

K: That's all I am saying. Don't reduce it to an instinct, sir.

*P8:* What was the joke you were going to tell us?

K: A man dies and meets his friend in heaven. They talk and he says, 'If I am dead, why do I feel so awful?'

# VARANASI

I WONDER WHY you are all here. Why have we all gathered here on the banks of the Ganga? If one asked that question seriously, what would be your answer? Is it merely that you have heard this man talk several times before, therefore you say, let's go and hear him? What is the relationship of what he says to what you do? Are they two separate things? — you just listen to what he has to say and carry on with your daily life? Have you understood our question?

We two, like two old friends sitting under a tree, are going to talk over together not some abstract, theoretical problems, but our daily life which is far more important. We have got so many problems: how to meditate, which guru to follow — if you are a follower — what kind of practice you should do, what kind of daily activity you should go through, and so on. And also, what is our relationship to nature — to all the trees, the rivers, the mountains, the plains and the valleys? What is our relationship to a flower, to a bird that passes by? And, what is our relationship with each other — not with the speaker but with each other — with your wife, with your husband, with your children, with the environment, with your neighbour, your community, the government, and so on? What is our relationship to all this? Or are we just isolated, self-concerned, intensely interested in our own way of life?

We are asking all these questions as true friends, not as a guru. The speaker has no intention whatsoever to impress you, to tell you what to do or to help you. Please bear this in mind right through the talks. He has no intention *whatsoever* to help you. I will tell you why, the reason, the logic of it. You have had a great many gurus, thousands of them, a great many helpers — Christian, Hindu, Buddhist, every kind of leader — not only political, but so-called religious. You have had leaders of the major kind and the minor. And where are you at the end of this long evolution?

We are supposed to have lived on this earth for a million years, and during that long evolution we have remained barbarians. We may be cleaner, quicker at communication, have better hygiene, transportation and so on, but morally, ethically and — if I may use that word — spiritually, we are still barbarians. We kill each other not only in war, but also by words, by gestures. We are very competitive. We are very ambitious. Each is concerned with himself. Self-interest is the dominant note in our life — concern with our own well-being, security, possessions, power, and so on. Aren't we concerned with ourselves — spiritually, religiously, in business? Right through the world we are all concerned with ourselves. That means isolating ourselves from the rest of humanity. That is a fact; we are not exaggerating. We are not saying something that is not true.

Wherever you go — the speaker has been all over the world and still goes round — what is happening? Increase in armaments, violence, fanaticism and the great, deep sense of insecurity, uncertainty and separateness — you and I — is a common note of mankind. Please, we are facing facts, not theories, not some kind of distant theoretical, philosophical statements. We are looking at facts. Not *my* facts as opposed to *your* facts but facts. Every country in the world, as you must all know, is gathering armaments — every country, however poor, however rich. Right? Look at your own country — the immense poverty, disorder, corruption, you all know that, and the gathering of armaments. It used to be a club to kill another, now you can vaporize mankind by the million with one atom bomb or neutron bomb. An immense revolution is going on, of which we know very little. The technological process is so rapid, that overnight there is something new. But ethically we are what we have been for a million years. You understand the contrast? Technologically we have the computer which will out-think man, which can invent new meditations, new gods, new theories. And man — that is, you and I — what is going to happen to our brains? The computer can do almost anything that human beings can, except, of course, have sex or look at the new moon. This is not some theory; it is happening now. So, what is going to happen to us as human beings?

We want entertainment. Probably this is part of your idea of entertainment, coming here, sitting listening and agreeing or disagreeing, and going back home to carry on with your life; it's a part of entertainment, as going to church, the temple, the mosque, or football or cricket in this country. Please, this is not an entertainment. You and I, the speaker, must think together, not just sit quietly and absorb some strange atmosphere, some *punya*; sorry, it is not like that at all.

We are going to think together sanely, logically, look at the same thing together. Not how *you* look and *I* look, but together observe our daily life, which is far more important than anything else — observe it every minute of our day. So first we are going to think together, not merely listen, agree or disagree, which is very easy. One wishes strongly that you could put aside agreement and disagreement! That is very difficult for most people who are too eager to agree or disagree. Our reactions are so quick, we classify everything — religious man, irreligious man, mundane, and so on. So if you could, this morning at least, put aside completely agreement and disagreement and merely observe together, think together. Will you do it? — Put aside altogether your opinion and my opinion, your way of thinking and the other person's way of thinking and merely observe together, think together.

Agreement and disagreement divide people. It is illogical to say, 'Yes, I agree with you' or, 'I do not agree with you', because you are either projecting, holding on to your opinion, your judgement, your evaluation, or discarding what is said. So could we this morning, just for amusement, for entertainment if you like, forget our opinions, our judgements, our agreements or disagreements and have a good clear brain — not devotional or emotional or romantic, but a brain that does not get involved in all the complications of theory, opinion, admission and dissension. Could we do that?

So let us proceed. What is thinking? Every human being in the world, everyone from the most ignorant, most crude, from the very, very small person in a little village to the most highly sophisticated scientist, has something in common — thinking. We all think — the villager who has never read anything, never been to a school, college or university, and most of you here who have been educated. The man who sits in the Himalayas by himself, he also thinks. And this thinking has been going on right from the beginning. So you must first ask the question: what is thinking? What is it that you think about? Will you answer that question first — not from books, not from the Gita or the Upanishads or the Bible or the Koran.

What is thinking? We live by thinking. Our daily action is based on thinking. You may think one way, and another may think another way, but it is still thinking. So, what is it? Can you think if you have no memory? Can you think backwards and forward, — what you will do tomorrow or the next hour, or what you have done yesterday or this morning? — which in the technological world of the computer is called architecture. So we must find out, together, not the Indian way of thinking or the European way of thinking, or the particular way of thinking of the Buddhist, the Hindu, the Muslim, the Christian or any other sect, but what is thinking. Unless we really understand the process of thinking, our life is always going to be very, very limited. So, we must very deeply, seriously, examine this whole process of thinking which shapes our life. Man has created god by his thinking; god has not created man. It must be a very poor god who created these human beings who are fighting each other perpetually. So, what is thinking and why have we made problems of it?

Why do we have problems in our life? We have plenty of them — political problems, financial problems, economic problems, the problems of one religion against another, problems by the thousands. What is a problem and what is the meaning of the word problem? According to the dictionary, it means something thrown at you, a challenge, something you've got to look at, face. You can't dodge it, you can't run away from it, you can't suppress it; it's there like a sore thumb. Why is it that all our life, from the moment we are born till we die, we have problems — about death, about fear, about a hundred things? Are you asking this question, or am I asking it for you? From the moment you are born you have problems. You go to school — there, you have to read, write, and that becomes a problem to the child. A little later he has to learn mathematics, and that becomes a problem. And the mother says, 'Do this, and don't do that,' and that becomes a problem. So from childhood we are bred in problems, our brain is conditioned in problems; it's never free from problems. As you grow, become adolescent, have sex, learn how to earn money, whether to follow society or not — all this becomes a problem. And in the end you yield to society, to the environment. Every politician in the world solves one problem and thereby creates other problems. Haven't you noticed all this? The human brain — what is inside this skull — itself has problems. So can the brain ever be free of problems to solve problems? Do you understand my question? If the brain is not free of problems, then how can it solve any problem? This is logical. Right? So, your brain, which carries memories, which has acquired tremendous industrial knowledge, has been nurtured, educated, to have problems. We are asking now if that brain can be free of problems first, so that it can then solve problems. Can you be free of problems first? Or is that impossible? Our brain is conditioned in the various narrow religions; it is conditioned by specialization, by the environment in which we live, by our education, by poverty or richness, by the vows you have taken as monks. (I do not know why, but you have taken them and it becomes a torture, a problem.) So our brains are extraordinarily conditioned as businessman, housekeeper, and so on. And from that narrow point of view we look at the world.

So we have to go into this question not only of having problems but also of what is thinking. Why do we think at all? Is there a different way of action? Is there a different manner of approaching life, of daily living, that doesn't require thinking at all? First, we'll have to look very closely, together; find out for ourselves, and then act. So, we are going to go into that. What is thinking? If you didn't think, you would not be here. You have made arrangements to come here at a certain time, and you have also made arrangements to go back. That is thinking. What is thinking philosophically? Philosophy means the love of truth, the love of life — not passing some examination at a university. So let us find out, together, what is thinking.

If you had no memory of yesterday, no memory at all of any kind, would you think? Of course not — you can't think if you have no memory, right? So what is memory? You did something yesterday, and that is registered in the brain, and according to that memory you think and act. You remember somebody flattering you, remember somebody hurting you, saying ugly things about you. That is, memory is the outcome of knowledge. Now, what is knowledge? This is rather difficult. We all accumulate knowledge; the great scholars, the great professors, scientists, acquire tremendous knowledge. So what is knowledge? How does it come about? Knowledge comes when there is experience. You are in an accident in a car — that becomes an experience. From that experience you have knowledge. And from that knowledge you have memory. From memory you have thought. Right? So, what is experience? It is that incident, the accident in a car, which is registered in the brain as knowledge. Experience, knowledge, memory, thought: this is logical — not my way of looking at it or your way of looking at it.

So, all experience, whether it is god's experience or your experience, is limited. The scientists are adding to it more and more every day, and that which is added to is always limited, right? I know little, and I must know more — you are adding. Your experience of something is always limited as there's something more to be added. So experience is limited, knowledge is limited — for ever. Therefore, memory is limited, and so thought is limited, right? And where there is limitation, there is division — as the Sikh, the Hindu, the Buddhist, the Muslim, the Christian, the democrat, the republican, the communist. They're all based on thought, and therefore all the governments are limited, all your activity is limited. Whether you think most abstractly or try to be very noble, it is still thinking, right? So, from that limited quality of thinking, as thinking is always limited, our actions are limited. Now, from that you begin to enquire very carefully: can thought have its right place and have no other place at all? You understand my question? So, is there an action which is free of limitation? That is, thinking being limited, we have reduced the whole universe into a very small affair. We have made our life into such a small affair, like thinking — I must be this, I must not be that, I must have power. You follow? We have reduced the enormous quality of life into a very small, petty little affair.

So, is it possible to be free of thought? Which means, I must think to come here; if I am a bureaucrat, I must think in terms of bureaucracy; if I go to the factory and turn the screw, I must have certain knowledge. Why should I have knowledge about myself? — the higher self, lower self and all that? Why should I have knowledge about that? It's very simple — it's self-interest; I'm only concerned with myself actually. We may pretend to have brotherhood, we may talk about peace, play with words, but we're always self-centred. So, from that arises the question: With this self-centredness, which is essentially deep selfishness, can there be a change at all? Can we be utterly selfless? So we have to enquire: what is the self?

What are you apart from your name and profession, your vows, following some guru? What are you? Or I'll put it another way — are you your name, are you your profession, are you part of the community, part of the tradition? Don't repeat what the Geeta says, what the Upanishads say or somebody says; that's futile. *Actually*, what are you? Is this the first time this question has been put to you — what are you? Aren't you your fear, aren't you your name, aren't you your body? Aren't you what you think you are, the image you have built about yourself? Aren't you all that? Aren't you your anger? Or is the anger separate from you? Come on, sirs, aren't you your fears, your ambitions, your greed, your competition, your uncertainty, your confusion, your pain, your sorrow — aren't you all that? Aren't you the guru you follow? So, when you identify yourself with that, aren't you all that? Or are you something higher up — superself, superconsciousness? If you say you have super-consciousness, a higher self, that's also part of thinking; therefore, what you call higher thinking, higher self, is still very small.

So, what are you? I'm saying, you're a bundle of all that is put together by thought. Whatever you think, you are. You may invent all kinds of stuff, but that invention too is what you are. Right? Putting it all together it is called me, myself, my ego, my personality, my higher self, my god. And I invent all this kind of stuff. Who has put all this together? Or is there only one structure? Who has divided all this? Who has said I'm a Hindu or I'm a Muslim? Is it merely propaganda? Who created the division between countries? Thought? Or is it desire, the longing to be identified, to be safe?

I'm asking you most respectfully, who has created this division? Is it thought? Of course, but behind thought there is something else. Who is doing all this, apart from thought? What is the desire, what is the urge, what is the movement behind it? Security, isn't it? I want to be secure; that's why I follow a guru. I want to be secure in my relationship with you, with my wife — she is *my* wife, — secure, protected, safe. The desire, the urge, the response, the reaction, is for safety — I must be safe, secure.

We all want security, but we never question: is there security at all? Is there any place where I can say I'm safe? You distrust your wife, your wife distrusts you. You distrust your boss because you want his place. It is all commonsense. You may laugh at it now but each human being in the world wants to have a place where he can be safe, secure, where there is no competition, where he is not pushed around, where he is not harassed. Don't you want all that? But you never ask: is there security at all? If you want security, you must also ask the question: Is there security at all?

Then the question arises: Why do you want security? Is there security in your thinking? Is there security in your relationship — with your wife and with your children? Is there security in your job? You may be a professor, carefully protected, but there are higher professors; so you want to become the vice-chancellor. So where is security? There may be no security at all. Just think about it, sir, see the beauty of that — having no desire for security, having no urge, no feeling of any kind in which there is security. In your homes, in your offices, in your factories, in your parliaments and so on, is there security? Life may not have security; life is meant to be lived, not to create problems and then try to solve them. It's meant to be lived, and it will die. That's one of our fears — to die, right?

So, this morning, have we learned from each other — not helped each other — have we learned, have we heard at all what the speaker is talking about? Have you heard with the ear, seen the facts of the world which is you — for the world is you? Or are they all ideas? There is a difference between fact and idea; the idea is never the fact. The *word* 'microphone' is not *the* microphone, this thing in front of the speaker. But we have made the word the thing. So the Hindu is not you — the *word* is not you. You are the *fact*, not the word. So, can we see the word and see that the word is not the thing? The word 'god' is not god. The word is different, totally, from the reality.

So, we are asking most respectfully: what have you learned this morning, *actually* learned, so that you will act, not say yes, quite right, and go home and carry on as before. The world is in great chaos. I don't know if you realize it; there is great trouble in the world, great misery. You are confused, therefore you are creating all this in the world around you. If you don't alter yourself, the world cannot alter, change. Because, in the world, everywhere you go, every human being goes through the same phenomenon as you are going through — uncertain, unhappy, fearful, insecure, wanting security, trying to control, saying that your guru is better than my guru, and so on. You understand, sir?

The speaker is not an optimist or a pessimist. We are presenting you with facts, not newspaper facts. We are talking together about *your* life, not the life of a guru, or an emperor, or somebody or other. We are talking together about your life. Your life is like that of the rest of the world. Human beings are terribly unhappy, uncertain, miserable, unemployed by the millions, in poverty, hunger, sorrow, pain, just like you; you're not different from them. You may call yourself Hindu or Muslim or Christian or what you like, but consciously, inwardly, you are just like the rest of the world. You may be dark brown, they may be light brown, have a different government, but every human being shares this terrible world. *We* have made the world — you understand? *We* are society. If you want society to be something different, *you* have to start, *you* have to bring order to your house, the house which is you.

# VARANASI

MAY WE GO on with what we were talking about yesterday? As we said, we are taking a long journey together, in a train, a very long journey, right throughout the world, and that journey began two and a half million years ago. During that long interval of time and distance, we've had a great many experiences, and those experiences are stored in our brain, either in the conscious or in the unconscious, deeper layers of it. And, together, you and the speaker are going to examine, explore. Not that the speaker alone talks — we're talking together. The speaker is putting it into words, and the words have a very significant meaning — not just the vocabulary, but the depth of the word, the significance of the word, the meaning of the word.

As you and the speaker are taking the journey together, you can't just go to sleep. You can't just say, 'Yes, I agree' or 'I disagree'. We went into that; we are not agreeing or disagreeing. We are merely looking out of the window, seeing what extraordinary things man has gone through, what experience, what pain, what sorrow, what unbearable things man has created for himself and for the world. We are not taking sides, pro and con, left, right or centre — please understand this very carefully.

This is not a political meeting, this is not an entertainment; this is a serious gathering. If you want to be entertained, you should go to a cinema or a football match. This is a very serious meeting as far as the speaker is concerned. He has talked all over the world: unfortunately or fortunately he may have created a reputation, and probably you are coming here because of that reputation, but that has no value at all. So, we are going to examine together, sitting together in that train, taking an infinitely long journey. We are not trying to impress you, we are not trying to force you to look at something.

We are looking at our daily life and all the background of a million years. One must listen to all the whispers, hear every moment, see everything as it is — not as you would wish it to be but actually what you see out of the window of the train as it goes along — the hills, the rivers, the stretch of water and all the beauty around you. Shall we talk about beauty for a while? Would it interest you? It's a very serious subject, like everything in life. Probably you have never asked what beauty is. For the moment we are going to enquire into what it is because you are passing in that train the most wonderful scenery — the hills, the rivers, the great snow-clad mountains, deep valleys, and not only things outside you, but also the inward structure and nature of your own being — what you think, what you feel, what your desires are. One has to listen to all this — not only to our own inward thoughts, feelings, and our opinions and judgements, but also to the sound of what other people are saying — what your wife is saying, what your neighbour is saying; listen to the sound of that crow, feel the beauty of the world, the beauty of nature. Not just say yes, right, wrong, this is what I think, this is what I should not think, or merely follow some tradition, but very quietly, without any reaction, see the beauty of a tree.

So together, we're going to talk about beauty. What is beauty? Have you been to museums, some of you? Probably not. I won't take you around the museums; I am not a guide. But instead of looking at the pictures, and statues of the ancient Greeks, ancient Egyptians, Romans and the moderns, we are looking, asking, inquiring, demanding to find out what is beauty. Not the form, not a woman or a man or a small child that is extraordinarily beautiful — all children are — but what is beauty? I'm asking the question, sir. Please answer it to yourself first, or have you never thought about it? Not the beauty of a face, but the beauty of a green lawn, of a flower, of the great mountains with the snow covering them, and the deep valleys, and the still tranquil waters of a river. All that is outside you and you say, 'How beautiful that is!' What does that word 'beauty' mean? It's very important to find that out, because we have so little beauty in our daily life. If you go through Benares you will know all about it — the filthy streets, the dust, the dirt. And seeing all this, as also the tenderness of a leaf or the tender generosity of human beings, you enquire deeply about this word that is used by poets, painters and sculptors, as you are asking yourself now. What is this quality of beauty? Do you want me to answer it or will you answer it? The gentleman says, you answer it because we don't know. Why? Why don't you know? Why haven't we enquired into this enormous question? You have your own poets, from the ancient people to now. They write about it, they sing about it, they dance, and you say you don't know what beauty is. What a strange people you are!

So, what is beauty? The same question put in different words is what are you? What is the nature and structure of you, apart from the biological factor? That is very closely related to what is beauty. When you look at a mountain, snow-capped, deep valleys, blue, deep hills, what do you feel, what's your real response to all that? Aren't you, for a second or for a few minutes, absolutely shocked by it, by the greatness, the immensity of the green valley, the extraordinary light and the blue sky against the snow-clad mountains? What happens to you at that moment when you look at that — the grandeur, the majesty of those mountains? What do you feel? Do you, for the moment, or for a few minutes, exist

at all? You understand my question? Please don't agree; look
at it very closely. At that moment when you look at
something grand, immense, majestic, for a second you don't
exist — you've forgotten your worries, your wife and your
children, your job, all the messiness of your life. At that
moment you are stunned by it. For that second, the grandeur
has wiped out all your memory, just for a second, and then
you come back. What happens during that second when *you*
are not there?

That is beauty — you understand? — when *you* are not
there. With the grandeur, the majesty of a mountain or a
lake, or that river early in the morning making a golden path,
for a second you've forgotten everything. That is, when the
self is not, there is beauty. Where *you* are not, with all your
problems and responsibilities, your traditions and all that
rubbish, then there is beauty. Like a child with a toy, as long
as the toy is complex and he plays with it, the toy absorbs
him, takes him over. The moment the toy is broken, he's
back to whatever it was he was doing. We are also like that.
We are absorbed by the mountain; it's a toy for us for a
second, or for a few minutes; then we go back to our world.
And we are saying, without a toy, without being absorbed by
something greater, can you be free of yourself? You understand my question? You don't understand this; you're too
clever; you are covered with a lot of knowledge, experience,
and so on. That's what's the matter with all of you — too
much learning. You're not simple enough. If you are very
simple, deeply simple in yourself, you will discover something extraordinary.

We have talked over beauty for a while. Now let us look at
ourselves. We have created the world — you, the speaker, his
forefathers, the past generations. What is it all about? —
killing each other, maiming each other, dividing: my god,
your god. Why is this society so ugly, so brutal, so cruel?
Who has created this monstrous world? I am not being

pessimistic or optimistic, but look at the world, the things that are going on outside of you: poor countries buying armaments, your country buying armaments, and immense poverty, competition — who has created all this? Will you say god has created it? He must be a messy god. So who created this society, who put it together? Haven't *you* put it together? Not only you, but your father, your great-grandfather, the past generations of a million years — they have created this society through their avarice, envy, competition. They have divided the world economically, socially, religiously. Face the facts, sir. We have put this society together, we are responsible for it — not god, not some external factors, but each one of us has created this society. You belong to this group and I belong to another group; you worship one god and I worship another god: you follow one guru and I follow another. So we have divided society, and we have divided it not only socially, but also religiously. Geographically we have divided the world — Europe, America, Russia; we have divided culture — western culture and eastern culture; we have divisions in government — socialist, democratic, republican, communist, and so on. You understand, sir, how our brain works? It divides, divides, divides. Haven't you noticed this fact? And out of this division comes conflict.

So you have created this society; you *are* this society. So, unless *you* change radically, you'll never change it. The communists have tried to change it, forcing man, secretly, viciously, to submit to various forms of compulsion. You must know all this: this is history. So where there is division, there must be conflict; that's the law. And apparently we like conflict, we live in perpetual conflict. So we must go back and find out what is the cause of all this. Is it desire? Is it fear? Is it pleasure? Is it the avoidance of all pain and therefore guilt? Let us begin to find out for ourselves what is desire. That is the basis — desire to have power, desire to achieve, desire to become somebody. We are not against desire, we are not trying to become somebody. We are not against desire, we are not trying to suppress desire or transcend desire, like the monks. We must, together, understand what is desire.

Are you interested to find out what is the root of desire? Do you want me to explain? But explanation is not the thing, the description is not *that*. When one describes a marvellous tree, the description is not the tree. We use words to convey something to each other, but the words, the descriptions, are not the fact. The *word* 'wife' is not the wife. If you can understand that simple fact, you will treat her better.

So, what is desire and why does it dominate us? What is its place, what is its nature? Monks the world over suppress desire or want to transcend desire or identify it with certain images, certain symbols, certain rituals. But what is desire? Have you ever asked that question? Or do you yield to desire, whatever the consequences?

We live by sensation, don't we? — better food, better house, better wife. Sensation is a part of life, so is sex — it's a sensation, a pleasure, and we have a great many pleasures, pleasure of possession and so on. Sensation is an extraordinarily important part of our existence. If you have no sensation you are dead, right? All your nerves go, your brain withers. We live by sensation, sensation being touch, feeling, like running a nail suddenly into your finger — that's sensation; you call it pain. Tears, laughter, humour are all part of sensation. You want more power, more money, and 'the more' is part of sensation. Every second, every response — intellectual, theoretical, philosophical — is part of sensation. We live by sensation — be clear on that — that is, by the senses responding: good taste, bad taste; it's bitter, it's sweet. Sensation is natural, it is inevitable, it is part of life.

What happens when you have a sensation? When you see something very beautiful — a car, a woman, a man, or a lovely house — what happens? You have seen that lovely house, seen the gardens, seen the beauty of the landscape, and how the house is built, with styled grace and a sense of dignity. Then thought comes along, makes an image of that sensation, and then says, 'I wish I had that house.' At that moment desire is born. When sensation is given a shape, a form, then, at that second, desire is born. When I see something I don't have, like a house or a car, then sensation becomes dominant. When thought gives it an image, when thought comes along and says, 'I wish I had it', at that moment desire is born. Right? You understand the subtlety of it, the depth of it? When thought gives a form, a structure, an image to sensation, at that second desire is born.

Now the question is, can sensation not be caught by thought, which is also another sensation? You understand, sir? After sensation, take time before thought gives it a shape — have an interval between sensation and thought giving it a shape. Do it, and you'll learn a lot from that. So I'm saying, when there is time in between sensation and thought — an interval, long or short — you'll understand the nature of desire. In that there is no suppression, no transcending. Sir, if you drive a car, not knowing the mechanism of it, you are always a little nervous that something might go wrong. But if you have dismantled that car and put it together very carefully, known all the parts, then you're master of the machinery, then you're not afraid, for you can put it together again. So, if you understand the nature of desire, the way desire begins, then you are not afraid of it, then you know what to do with it.

There's something else which you and the speaker should talk over together. We have lived for thousands of years, and we have never understood the nature of fear. What is the source of fear, what is the cause of fear? We have apparently never ended fear — biological fear as well as psychological fear, inward fear — fear of death, fear of not having, not possessing, fear of loneliness — we have so many fears. Out of these fears you create gods, you create rituals, spiritual hierarchies, gurus, all the temples of the world. And we're asking, what is fear? Not your particular form of fear, not my fear and your fear, but fear? As I said, if you understand the machinery of a car, you're not afraid of it. So if you know, realize, understand the nature of fear, the cause of it, the root of it, then you will transcend fear, and fear is gone. We are going to do that this morning.

We are asking, what is fear, what is the cause of it — not how to end it, not how to transcend it, control it, suppress it, and run away from it, as you're doing, but what is the cause, the source of it? Think it out, sir, go into it for a minute. Take your fear, your particular fear, or fears; what is the root of them? — security? desire for more? If you haven't found it, you ask somebody like the speaker what the cause is. Will you listen?

Will you actually listen? I will explain, but the explanation is not the thing. Does the word 'fear' evoke fear in you? Fear is a fact; the word is not the fact. So the explanation is not a means to end fear. We have to examine then what is time, because time is fear: tomorrow something might happen, my house might fall down, my wife might turn to another man, my husband might go off — and I'm in fear. Fear of the past, fear of the future, fear of the present: I have been that, I won't be that, but I am not that now — that whole process is a movement in time. From here to there is a movement, and it needs time. All movement is time.

The past shapes the present. The past is operating now, and the future is shaped by the present — modified. Circumstances change, certain incidents happen, so the past is modified, changed, altered, and the future is what happens now. All time — the past, the present and the future — is contained in the *now*. This applies to life; it is not just a theory. You were something yesterday; an incident takes place today that changes, modifies, slightly alters the past, and the future is what you are now, modified. That is, the past, the present and the future are now; tomorrow is now. If there is no mutation *now*, you'll be exactly the same as you've been before. I think I am a Hindu, with all the circus romp behind it, and I'll be a Hindu tomorrow. That is logical. Therefore what you do now matters much more than what you will do tomorrow. So, what are you going to do if tomorrow is now? That is a fact; it is not my theory or your theory, it's a fact. I am greedy now, and if I don't do anything about it now, I'll be greedy tomorrow. Can you stop being greedy today? Will you? No, of course not. So you will be what you have been. This has been the pattern of humanity for millions of years.

You don't mind killing. Be honest. You don't mind killing, you subscribe to it, you want your country to be strong. Right? Don't be ashamed of it — this is a fact. And so you gather armaments. If you don't stop being an Indian now, you'll be an Indian tomorrow. So I'm asking, what will you do *now*? Stop being an Indian, will you? Do you know what the implications are? — not the passport, not the paper — but not being associated with *any* religion, *any* group; they are all phoney anyhow. Is that possible? Will you do it? Do you see that if there is no mutation now, *today*, you'll be exactly the same tomorrow? This is not being optimistic or pessimistic; this is a fact. Do you understand the seriousness of it? If there is no radical mutation *now*, I'll be the same tomorrow.

So time is a factor in fear. And fear is a common factor of all mankind. Can that fear — not one branch of it — but the root of fear be totally demolished? — that is, to have no fear of *any* kind. The speaker says it is eminently possible; that it can be done radically. The speaker is saying that fear can be totally ended. Don't say it is for the illumined one and all that nonsense. You can end it if you put your brain, your heart into it — completely, not partially. And then you will see for yourself what immense beauty there is in it; a sense of utter freedom — not freedom of a country or of some government, but the sense of the enormity of freedom, the greatness of freedom.

Will you do it — today, now? From today, seeing the cause of fear, end it. As long as there is fear — biologically, physically, psychologically — it destroys us. So, if one may ask, after listening to this fact, not theory, what are you going to do? Time is the factor of fear and thought; so if you don't change now, you won't ever change. It is constant postponement.

# VARANASI

WE'RE GOING TO talk over together a great many things this morning, and, as we said, we're not the only speaker; you and the speaker are sharing all the issues that we are going to discuss. We are participating in them, not just listening casually. In the last two talks we've dealt with many things: fear and all the travail of man, the problems that we have, which we never seem to resolve; we went into that carefully. The problems exist because our minds are filled with problems; therefore there is no freedom to look at any problem. Also we went into the question of thought — why thought has made this life so utterly impossible. Thought has brought about a great deal of conflict, wars for two and a half million years, which means practically every year we kill each other — in the name of god, in the name of patriotism, my country against your country, our religion against your religion, and so on. And we also talked about the nature of thought, why thought divides men or brings them together to do a certain project, like going to the moon. To build that rocket, you probably had to have over 300,000 people, all of them doing their little job perfectly. Either we get together in a crisis like war which is born of hatred, or we come together on some national issue, or when there is a great calamity like an earthquake, or volcanic eruption. Apart from that, we never get together.

Now, this morning, if I may most respectfully suggest, we should all get together, as we are all sitting together, and gather energy so that we can think out very clearly the various issues we are going to raise together. That means to activate our brains which are rather sluggish, slow, monotonous, repetitive. So we are together keeping our brains alert. We have not only to keep the physical organism active because that gives energy, but to have a very clear, active brain. Not a specialized brain as a philosopher, as a scientist, as a physicist, and so on. Those specialized brains become very narrow. Philosophy, according to the dictionary, means the love of truth, the love of life, the love of wisdom — not just adding more and more theories or quoting somebody and explaining what they have quoted.

I don't know if you've ever gone into the question of learning, what it is to learn. Now we are going to find out together what it means. We generally take learning to mean memorizing. All through school, college and university you memorize. And that memory can be used to earn a livelihood, to gain power, possessions, prestige, patronage, and so on. Is there another kind of learning? We know the ordinary kind of learning — at school, college, university or learning a skill to become an excellent carpenter or a plumber or a cook. So, what is learning? Have you ever thought about it? When you're memorizing, your brain is filled with memories. That's simple. Memory multiplies, keeps you somewhat alert, you learn more and more and more. So the speaker is asking you — is there a different kind of learning altogether, which is not merely memorizing.

This is a very important question because the brain records every incident, every kind of memory. When you're hurt it is recorded, but you never enquire *who* is hurt; we'll come to that presently. So the brain is recording; see the importance of that. It has to record, otherwise you and I wouldn't be here. So the brain is constantly recording, discarding. Now, is it necessary to record? You have an incident in a car — an accident; it is instantly recorded, because you are hurt or your car is damaged. The brain has the capacity, the energy, not only to record but also to safeguard itself. And we are asking: is it necessary to record everything? Or can we record only that which is necessary and nothing else? Have you put this question to yourself? The brain records for its own security, otherwise you and I wouldn't be sitting here. You have recorded how long it took you to come here and so on. We're asking, is it necessary to record certain things, and totally unnecessary where the psyche is involved? You understand my question, sir? Is it necessary when you are flattered or when you're insulted to record it? Is it necessary to record these things?

The recording builds up the psyche. This is a very serious question. The psyche, which is made up of various elements, characteristics, ethos, is contained in the brain, which we call consciousness. In that consciousness, memories, fears, etc., are contained. So we're asking again, is it necessary to build up the psyche? The psyche means the self, the self being all the memories, the activities of thought, imagination, fascination, fear, pleasure, sorrow, pain. It is recording that makes up the whole psyche, the 'I', the persona.

So we're asking, Is it necessary to record so as to build up the self? Have you ever thought about this, looked at it or investigated it, gone into this question of recording as you would into various philosophical, religious matters? It may be necessary to record certain things and *totally unnecessary* to record others — see the beauty of it — so that the brain is not always conditioned in memory, so that the brain becomes extraordinarily free, but active. That is the first question.

So, learning is *not to record*. We have discussed this matter with psychiatrists in New York. They were fascinated with the idea of not recording, so that the brain cells themselves mutate. Our brains are built up of cells and so on — I'm not a professional — and in the brain cells are the memories. And we live on those memories — the past and all the remembrances that one has. And the older you get the more you go back, further and further, till you die. And it is important to learn to find out whether the brain needs to record everything. Forgetting, and not recording, are two entirely different matters. When you are hurt, not physically but psychologically, inwardly, you say 'I am hurt.' You are all hurt, aren't you? From childhood till you grow old and die, you are being hurt all the time. You say, 'I can't stand any more hurts, I've been hurt so much. I'm frightened.' I build a wall around myself, isolate myself — all these are the consequences of being hurt.

Now, who is being hurt? You say, 'It's me.' Then what is 'me'? You just say 'me', 'I', the ego, any word that comes, but you don't investigate who is the 'I', who is the persona. Who are you — a name, a degree if you are fortunate or unfortunate enough, a job, a house or a flat, and a title after a name? There are the images you have built about yourself, so that when you say you are hurt, the images about yourself are hurt. But all those images are you — you're a physicist, you're a doctor, you're a philosopher, you're an MP, or an engineer. Have you ever realized how someone is always introduced by his profession? So the self, the psyche, the persona, is the image which you have built about yourself.

You have built an image about your wife, and she builds an image about you — and these images have relationship. See what is happening. The *images* have relationship — not the persons but the images — and you live on that. So you never know your wife or your husband or your friend. Or you don't care to know, but you have the image. So the question is: can you live without a single image? See the implications of it, the beauty of it, the freedom of it.

We ought to talk over together why we make all this effort in life. Why do we make such an immense effort to do anything? We make tremendous efforts to meditate, to live, to fight, to battle with one another — opinion against opinion, judgement against judgement, I agree with you, I disagree with him. Why all this effort? For what? — for money, for your family, for affection, to feel that you must be loved by somebody?

When you ask that question, then you must ask, what is love? Is love effort? — I must love you, therefore I am going to make an effort about it. Can there be love when there is ambition? Sir, please, this is serious; this is not for somebody who doesn't care, who just wants his own way. Is love ambition, is it greed, is it self-centredness? Is love the opposite of hate?

You know, we have always been fighting — the good fighting the bad, all through life. You see it in paintings symbolizing the good and symbolizing the devil. In Greek mythology and other mythologies it is the white bull against the black bull or good fighting evil in different shapes, symbols and so on. We still do that — the good fighting the bad. Is the good separate from the bad? Is the good born out of the bad? If the good is related to the bad, then it's not good. If the good is born of, comes from, the bad, then it's not good. That is simple, isn't it? But if the bad is totally divorced from the good, if there is no relationship between the good and the bad, then there is only the bad and the good, totally divorced from each other. Therefore they can't fight.

So then we have to enquire, what is the good? And you have to ask, can love contain hate? Or, has hate nothing to do with love — therefore there is no relationship between the two, therefore they can't fight each other? This is an important question for you to understand, go into. You always say, 'I have not been good today, but I will be good tomorrow,' or, 'I have been angry today, but I will not be angry tomorrow.' This is the relative relationship between the good and the bad. Love has nothing whatsoever to do with jealousy; love has nothing whatsoever to do with hate. Where there is hate, pleasure, anxiety, and so on, love cannot exist. And the speaker questions whether you love anybody at all.

What is love? How does it come about? Do you really ask that question, or am I asking it for you? Can love exist where there is sorrow? Most of us are in sorrow of some kind or other — failing in an exam, failing to be successful in business, or in politics, or in your relationship with your wife, or in your relationship with somebody upstairs — which may be your guru or some other imaginative figure. So when you can't succeed you are depressed, you are sorrowful. Or you are sorrowful because you live in a small little village and you don't know how to read and write, you don't know how to drive a car, or you have no hot bath or you wear one dirty cloth. The man in a position high up on the ladder — he suffers too.

So, everyone on this earth — everyone — from the richest to the poorest, from the most powerful to the least powerful, suffers. Suffering is not *yours*, because everyone suffers. It's not *my* suffering; it's suffering. I wonder if you understand that? My son dies and I get terribly upset. I weep and I say, 'My god, I've lost my son,' and that becomes a perpetual problem. I weep every time I see a little boy or a little girl. And I go through the pain of loneliness, sorrow.

If there is sorrow, there is no love. Please realize this. If I suffer, suffer, suffer, it's part of self-pity, self-concern, it's: 'My sorrow is different from your sorrow', like 'My guru is stronger than your guru', or 'My god is different from your god'. So, is there an end to sorrow? Or must mankind go through this sorrow all its life? The speaker says it can end. Otherwise there is no love. I'm shedding tears all the time, I suffer, and you come along and tell me, 'Every human being on earth suffers; it is not your suffering, we all share it.' I refuse to accept such a statement because I love my sorrow, I'm happy in my sorrow, and I want to be separate in my sorrow.

To get a feeling of this requires a great deal of enquiry, persuasion, talking over, saying, 'It is not quite yours. Have a little bit of it, but it isn't quite yours'. That means no self-pity, and it means you are really sharing the burden of sorrow for all the rest of mankind. Go on, sir, think about it, look at it; you are part of humanity; you are not separate from humanity. You may have a better position, better degrees, better money, but you are part of mankind, your consciousness is part of mankind. Your consciousness contains all the things that you have thought about, imagined, feared, and so on. Your consciousness is that, and that is also the consciousness of mankind. Mankind has fear, sorrow, pain, anxiety, tears, uncertainty, confusion. Every human being on earth has all this, and you are like the rest. So you are not individuals. I know my body is different from your body — you are a woman, I'm a man. But we are in the world as one unit. When you feel that relationship, you are the rest of mankind. Then something totally different takes place, not just words, imaginings, but the feeling of it, the enormity of it.

We ought to talk about death. Sorry, on a lovely morning, sitting under the trees, quiet — no train crossing the bridge — to talk about death may seem morbid, may seem ugly. Now together, we're going to examine it, share it — not you just listening and I talking. So, what is death? Why are we so frightened of it? Why do we keep death for ten years later or twenty years later or a hundred years later? Then, you have not only to ask what is death and dying, but also what is living. What is your life? — office from nine to five, as a clerk, as a governor, a factory worker or whatever it is, for the rest of your life, except when you retire as a gaga old man. And your life is breeding children, sex, pleasure, pain, sorrow, anxiety, problem after problem — illness, doctors, caesarean operations, pain in giving birth. This is your life. Do you deny that? And you call this living. You support it, you enjoy it, you want more and more of it. Right? And you put death as many years away as possible. And in that distance of time you are building up the same pattern over and over. Your children, your grandchildren, all live in that same pattern which you call living.

So I say to myself, why not bring that which you call death into living? You can't take anything with you — not even all that your guru has said and all that you have tried to live up to, nor your furniture, your wife, your children, nor all the silver you have collected, all the money in the bank. So, as you cannot take anything with you, why not let life and death meet? You understand what I'm saying? Why not let death come today? Not suicide — I'm not talking about that. Why not be totally free of attachment now — which is death? Be totally detached — today, not tomorrow. Tomorrow is death. So, why can't I be free of my attachments *now* so that living and dying are together all the time? I wonder if you see the beauty of it. That gives you an immense sense of freedom. So living and dying are together, always. It's not something to be frightened about. If the brain can do that, then there is a totally different quality to the brain. It has no hooks, it has no sense of the past, the future, the present. It is *living* — it is really an endless way of living. That is, every day is a new day. Don't mistake what I'm talking about — the future is now.

There is no 'I shall be born again next life'. That is an idea to which you're attached. It gives you great comfort, but if you believe in reincarnation, then you must act rightly now, because next life you are going to pay for it or be rewarded. It's a very comforting idea, but it is meaningless. Because, if you act rightly now, righteousness has no reward. Righteousness is righteousness, not what you are going to get out of it. That is a merchandizing attitude, a mechanical attitude.

We should talk about religion. What is religion? Sir, this is one of the important questions in life. There are temples all over India, mosques all over the world, churches all over the world and their priests beautifully decorated, beautifully garbed, all medallions and so on. This has been one of the problems from the most ancient times: the priest and the king — the priest wanted power, the king also wanted power. But the priest was stronger because he was the one who wrote, read, and the king had to obey him because he was supposed to be the wiser man. And gradually the king said, 'This is not good enough,' and so there was a war between the priest and the king. This is historical; you will find it in different books.

The word 'religion' had a very complicated meaning at one time, but now it has become a symbol, a ritual, a superstition. Is this religion, or is religion something entirely different, something which has nothing to do with rituals, with symbols, because all these have been invented by man? Because priests wanted power, position, they put on new hats, new clothes and grew long beards or shaved their heads — and all this is called religion. To an ordinary, thoughtful, fairly intelligent man, it is rubbish, total rubbish. If he discards all that, really discards it totally, puts away being a Hindu with all its superstitions, symbols, worship, prayer, then he is a serious man; he is not a word-monger.

Sir, the speaker is not laying down the law. Let us talk about it, let us investigate, let us go into it together. Our brains are chattering all the time. Haven't you noticed it? — Chattering, chattering, chattering or imagining, perpetually in action. There is never a moment of silence. And silence is also repetition — 'Ram, Ram' or whatever you may repeat. When you repeat something mechanically, as you repeat the word, gradually the brain, through repetition, becomes dull and quiet; and that quietness is something marvellous to you. You think you've achieved some tremendous thing and you go around repeating this to others, and the poor gullible people say, 'Yes, yes'. Your meditation is a series of achievements. Can you discard all that nonsense? For the speaker it is complete nonsense, it is like going to the circus.

We have to enquire what is meditation and what is silence. Silence allows space. You can't be silent in time. We have to go into this question of meditation, space, time, and whether there is an ending to time. We are not telling you how to meditate. Don't ask *how* to meditate. It is like telling a carpenter how to build a beautiful cabinet. If he is a good carpenter, you don't have to tell him. Your meditation now is achievement.

The word 'meditation' means 'to ponder over, think, weigh, look at carefully'. It also means 'to measure', from *ma* in Sanskrit. When you compare — 'I was this today, I'll be that tomorrow' — that is measurement. Measurement has no place in meditation. Measurement is necessary in all technologies — whether you build a chair or the most complicated rocket to go to the moon.

We are saying, meditation implies total freedom from all comparison and measurement — and this is difficult. Meditation is something that is marvellous if you know what to do. The meditator is different from meditation. As long as you are the meditator, there is no meditation, because the meditator is concerned about himself — how he is progressing, what he is doing. In meditation there is no meditator at all. See for yourself the beauty, the depth, the subtlety of it. The practice of meditation is not meditation — sitting and making the mind more and more dull, and saying, 'Yes, I've spent an hour.' (By the way, sir, don't touch my feet — that's most undignified, as a human being. You can hold my hand, but not the feet; it's inhuman, undignified.)

So meditation is something that cannot be practised as you practise a violin, a piano. To practise means you want to reach a certain level of perfection. But in meditation there is no level, nothing to be achieved. Therefore there is not a conscious, deliberate meditation; it is a meditation which is totally undirected, totally — if I may use the word — 'unconscious'. It is not a deliberate process. Let's leave it at that. We can spend a lot of time on this — an hour, a whole day, the whole of your life to find this out.

Now let us talk about space. Because meditation is that — space. We have no space in the brain. There is space between two struggles, between two thoughts, but it is still within the sphere of thought. So, what is space? Does space contain time? Or does time include all space? We talked about time. If space contains time, then it is not space. Then it is circumscribed, limited. So, can the brain be free of time? Sir, this is such an important, immense question; you don't seem to gather it.

If life, all of life, is contained in the *now*, do you see what it means? All humanity is you. All humanity — because you suffer, he suffers; his consciousness is you; your consciousness, your being, is him. There is no you and me that limits space. So, is there an end to time — not to the clock which you wind and it stops, but to the whole movement of time?

Time is movement, a series of incidents. Thought is also a series of movements. So time is thought. So we are saying, if space contains time, it is not space. So, is there an end to time? Which means, is there an end to thought; which means, is there an end to knowledge; is there an end to experience? — which is total freedom. And *this* is meditation. Not sitting and looking — that's childish. This demands not only a great deal of the intellect, but insight. The physicist, the artist, the painter, the poet and so on have a limited insight. We are talking about a timeless insight. This is meditation, this is religion, and this is the way to live, if you want to, all the rest of your days.

# VARANASI

KRISHNAMURTI (K): This is supposed to be a conversation between us. You are going to question me, question the speaker; we are going to have a discussion, a deliberation, take counsel together, weigh together, consider together, balance things together. It is not that one person answers your question or your queries; not that the speaker considers and then you agree — that is rather childish — but, rather, we are going to have a conversation together. Probably, you are not used to this — really to talk to somebody openly, frankly; probably you never do, even to your wife or husband or somebody closely related. You put on your mask, you pretend. If you could, put aside all that this morning and consider what questions we have, what we would like to talk over together, what you are most concerned with; not just some absurd stuff, but rather, what you really want to find out.

Before we begin to discuss — how do you approach a question? You understand what I am asking? How do you regard a question, a problem; how do you weigh the problem; how do you come very close to the problem? We cannot expect the speaker to answer your question because in the question itself may be the answer. Do you understand? So, whatever the question we are going to discuss this morning, let us examine it first, not wait for an answer. Have we understood this fact, or is it mysterious?

I have got a question for you — I am not going to answer it — Why do you separate living? our daily living from your

ideas of the spiritual? Why do you divide the two? Why do
you separate the so-called religious life and the monotonous,
lonely, daily life? You answer my question.

*First participant (P1):* Because it needs a different kind of
energy. The spiritual life and the ordinary, mundane life
involve two different kinds of energy.

K: That is, two different kinds of energy — one for the
so-called spiritual, religious life, and another kind of energy
for the mundane life. Now, I am not going to answer the
question. Let us find out if what you are saying is a fact.

You say that those people who are religious, who put on
those funny robes, need a kind of energy quite different from
that of a man who travels around and makes money or of the
poor man in the village. Why do you divide the two? May I
put that question? Energy is energy, right? — whether it be
electrical energy or motor-driven energy or solar energy or
the energy of a river in flood. So why do you divide energy? Is
it that the man with a beard, strange clothes, has more
energy, or that he is trying to concentrate his energy on a
particular issue? You understand, sir?

*P2:* There are various kinds of energy: one is the energy of
thought, which can be stilled; there is another, the energy of
insight, which does not get stilled, and there is yet another,
the energy of mind, which brings about compassion and
other things.

K: Certainly not.

*P2:* Pardon, sir?

K: Sir, we are talking it over, I am not laying down the law.
Would you mind listening.

*P2:* What is the relationship of the three aspects of energy, of
thought, of insight, and of mind?

K: You answer it.

*P3:* May I, sir?

K: Why not? You have a right to answer him.

*P3:* Just because we want to be comfortable, we divide energy into various compartments. I do not think there can be many types of energy. Energy can be only one.

K: Yes, I should have thought so myself. You see how we divide everything. We divide spiritual energy, mental energy, the energy of insight, the energy of thought.

*P3:* Then it gets so complicated.

K: I know it complicates it, doesn't it? Why not be very simple? The energy of the body, the energy of sex, the energy of thought, it is all energy. It is one thing; only we divide it. Why? Find out, madam, why do we divide it?

*P4:* We are conditioned to divide it.

K: Yes, sir. Why are you conditioned? Why do you accept this division? India-Pakistan, Russia-America — why do you divide all this? Tell me.

*P5:* The division is a reality.

K: Of course it is a reality. Why do you make obvious statements, sir?

*P5:* There is a difference between the truth and the reality.

K: All right, what do you call reality?

*P5:* What we see.

K: Therefore, you say that reality is right in front of you, right? — It is what you see visually, optically. Is the tree a reality?

*P5:* Yes, sir.

K: All right, is what you *think* a reality?

*P5:* Sometimes we have to think.

K: Is your wife a reality? I am asking you a question: what do you mean by 'my wife'?

*P6:* There is the psychological attitude that I have towards my wife and there is the reality of my wife who has her own psychology.

K: Are you saying, sir — if I may put it in my own words — that the image of your wife, the image which you have built up, is different from your wife; is that it?

*P6:* It may happen sometimes that the image coincides with the reality of what my wife is.

K: Have you looked at your wife? Have you seen her, enquired into her ambitions, her anxiety, the pain of bearing children and all the rest of it? Have you considered what the wife is? You have built an image about her, haven't you?

*P6:* Not necessarily.

K: I do not say necessary or unnecessary. It is a fact that you, if you are married, or if you have some friend, build an image about her? Don't you? Not necessarily, but it takes place, right?

*P6:* Yes, sir.

K: I am not trying to brow-beat you, sir, but each one has an image about the other. You have an image about me, otherwise you would not be here. So we create an image about another, depending on our temperament, depending on our knowledge, depending on our illusions, depending on our fantasies, and so on. We build an image about people: you have an image about the prime minister, you have an image about the person who is speaking to you. So we are asking a much deeper question, which is: can you live a daily life without images?

*P7:* The images that we build up are generally in relationship with ourselves. I build up an image around me.

K: Yes, you have an image about yourself.

*P7:* Yes, and if we can achieve that state which you have been talking about — effacing the centre, the self — then the images would automatically drop. Then one can live without the image.

K: So, when you talk about relationship, what do you mean by that word? Sir, please, just listen quietly before you answer. Take a little breather. What is your relationship with another? You understand the word 'relationship'? To be related — I am related to him through blood: he is my father, my brother, whatever it is. What do you mean by that word 'relationship'? Carefully, sir, do not be so quick; go slowly.

*P7:* I am not using the word 'relationship' in that sense.

K: I am talking in that sense.

*P8:* My care and concern for my friends, for my parents, for my children, including hatred — all that is included.

K: Do you really care? Or is it just an idea that you should care? If I may politely ask you, what do *you* mean by the word 'related' — not what meaning you *give* to it, the meaning according to the dictionary.

*P9:* Contacts through the actual, not through words or images.

K: Sir, I am asking you a question; do not kick it around. What do you mean by related? I am related to him — what does that mean?

*P10:* I think when I say I am related, I become a part of that.

K: Are you a part of your wife?

*P10:* Yes, partially.

K: Not total or partial. I am asking, what do you mean by the word 'related'?

*P11:* Sir, being associated with day-to-day life, a network of expectations from each other, duties and obligations.

K: Oh, God, you make it so very complex, don't you? I am just asking you what you mean by that word *per se* — for itself — not what you think it should be.

*P12:* Close touch; getting attached; to have something in common. If I have an image about you, then I have a relationship with you.

K: Do you have a relationship with me?

*P12:* Yes.

K: In what way? I am asking this seriously, sir; do not throw it aside.

*P12:* When I am looking at you without an image, I have relationship at that moment with you.

K: You really have not thought about it, sir. You are just throwing out words.

*P13:* I think we have diverted from the original question.

K: I know, I know. So, sir, let us go back. I will come back to this word; it is a very important word in our life.

Why do we divide the spiritual and the mundane? We divide India against Pakistan; we divide various religions — Christianity, Buddhism, Hinduism and so on; we divide, divide, divide. Why? Do not answer; just look at it, sir. We are taking counsel together; we are looking at the same problem together — why do we divide? Of course, there is a division between man and woman; or, you are tall, I am short; you are brown or white, I happen to be black — but that is natural, isn't it? I won't go into all that. So why do we divide?

*P14:* Because we have different ideas and different feelings and different interests, and we want to stick to them.

K: Why do you want to stick to them?

*P14:* Because we are selfish and we have self-interest.

K: Do not reduce everything to selfishness. Why do we divide, I am asking. Who is dividing?

*P15:* The mind itself first divides into the inner perception and then the outer perception.

K: Sir, is that your own experience, or are you quoting somebody?

*P15:* Half-half.

K: Could we please be serious for a while and face these facts? Why have we divided the world around us — Pakistan, India, Europe, America, Russia and so on? Who has made all these divisions?

*P16:* I think it is ego, it is thought.

K: Are you guessing? Why don't we look at the facts first? We have different ideologies, different beliefs: one section of the world believes in Jesus, the other section believes in Allah, some other section believes in the Buddha, another section believes in something else; who has made all these divisions?

*P17:* It is we, mankind.

K: That means you.

*P17:* Yes, sir.

K: You have divided the world.

*P17:* Yes, sir.

K: Why? Why have you divided it?

*P18:* Fear and security.

K: Are you sure of what you are saying?

*P19:* We divide ourselves because we derive pleasure from this division.

K: If you are being killed by the other party, is that also pleasure? Don't make casual remarks because this is not an entertainment; I am not here to entertain you.

So if you will kindly listen, I am asking you a question: who has divided the world into this? Has not man done this? You have done it — because you are a Hindu or a Muslim or a Sikh or some other sect, right? Man wants security, so he says, I belong to the Buddhists: that gives me identity, that gives me strength, that gives me a sense of place where I can stay. Why do we do this? Is it for security; because if I lived as a Hindu in a world of Muslims, they would kick me around? Or if I lived as a Protestant in Rome, I would find it awfully difficult because Rome is the centre of Catholicism, right? Who has done all this — made this colossal mess? You have done it, he has done it, she has done it. What will you do about it? Just talk about it? You don't want to act; you say, Let us carry on.

*P20:* You have no intention to help us but, when we are here, we find that you help us. How does that happen?

K: Too bad. I do not want to help anybody. It is wrong to help another, except surgically, with food, and so on. The speaker is not your leader; we have said it a thousand times all over Europe, America and here.

*P20:* You may not help us, but you make us understand things.

K: No! We are having a conversation together. In that conversation we may begin to see things clearly for ourselves. Therefore nobody is helping you; it is a conversation.

*P21:* Yes, sir.

K: Don't say, 'Yes sir'. Did you hear what I said — that the speaker is not here to help you in any way? He is not your guru, you are not his follower. The speaker says all that is an abomination.

*P22:* Why is there so much cruelty in nature that one being has to eat another in order to survive?

K: A tiger lives on smaller things, right? So the big things eat little things. And you are asking why nature is so cruel.

*P22:* No, sir. Why is there so much cruelty in nature?

K: First of all, why is there so much cruelty in nature? — that is natural, perhaps. Don't say there is cruelty in nature. Why are *you* so cruel? Why are human beings cruel?

*P23:* I want to get rid of my pain and sorrow; therefore, if anybody hurts me, I also react or respond in a similar manner.

K: Sir, have you ever considered that all human beings suffer — all human beings in the world, whether they live in Russia, America, China, India, Pakistan, wherever it is? All human beings suffer.

*P23:* Yes, sir.

K: Now, how do you solve that suffering?

*P23:* I am interested in my own suffering.

K: What are you doing about it?

*P23:* I have come here to be enlightened by you.

K: What shall we do together, sir, *together*? Not I help you or you help me; what shall we do together to get rid of sorrow?

*P23:* I don't know, sir.

K: Are you sure?

*P23:* Yes, sir.

K: No, no, answer carefully; this is a very serious question. Are you sure you don't know how to be free of sorrow?

*P23:* Yes, sir. I do not know how to get rid of my sorrow.

K: Just a minute, just a minute — remain in that state. Would you listen sir, please? He said a very serious thing. He said, 'I really don't know how to be free of sorrow.' When you say, 'I don't know,' is it that you are waiting to know? You understand my question?

*P23:* Yes, sir.

K: I don't know but I may be expecting some kind of answer. Therefore when I am expecting, I step out of not knowing.

*P23:* What does it mean — stay in not knowing?

K: I will tell you what it means; I am not helping you. It is a very serious matter when you say I am not helping you, because we have been helped for so many thousands of years. Sir, when you say 'I don't know,' what does that mean? I don't know what Mars is. He is an astro-physicist, and I go to him to find out what Mars is.

*P23:* But I am not interested in Mars.

K: I know you are not interested in Mars; nor am I. But I am taking that as an example. I don't know what Mars is, and I go to an astro-physicist and say, 'Sir, tell me what Mars is.' He tells me that Mars is various combinations of gas and all the rest of it, and I say, 'That is not Mars; your description of Mars is different from Mars.' So I ask you, when you say 'I don't know,' what do you mean by that — 'I don't know'? I am not waiting for an answer — which may be crooked, which may be false, which may be illusory, therefore I am not expecting, right? Are you in that state — 'I don't know'?

*P24:* We are stunned when we remain in that state.

K: Remain in that state. I don't know how to swim in the Ganga.

*P25:* I cannot do anything about it.

K: You cannot. When you do not know what is the cause of suffering, how it can be ended — you don't know, right? So remain in that state and find out. When you put a question you expect an answer, don't you? Be honest, be simple. You expect an answer from a book, from another person or from some philosopher — somebody to tell you the answer. Would you put a question and listen to the question? You understand what I am saying? When you put a question, would you wait for the question to reveal itself? I know if I can understand the question properly, I will find the answer. So the answer may be in the question.

That is, I put a question to you; don't try to find an answer, but find out if you have understood the question — the depth of the question or the superficiality of the question or the meaninglessness of the question. Would you look at the question first? So I am suggesting, sir, if you put a question to the speaker, the speaker says the question itself has vitality, energy, not the answer because the answer is in the question. Right? Find out. The question contains the answer.

*P26:* An intelligent mind can put a right question. I feel I am not intelligent at all so how can I ask a right question?

K: You cannot. But you can find out why you are not intelligent. He is intelligent, I am not. Why? Is intelligence dependent on comparison? You understand, sir? Did you listen to my question?

*P27:* Many times we find an answer to our question, but we require somebody else's approval of that answer.

K: So the answer is not important but the approval of another is important.

*P28:* The correct answer is important, and therefore approval of the correct answer is required.

K: By whom? By your friends, who are equally unintelligent? By whom do you want the approval — public opinion? the governor, the prime minister or high priests? From whom do you want approval, sir? You don't think at all; you just repeat, repeat.

*P29:* Sir, I remain with the situation 'I don't know', but it is tiresome.

K: Why is it tiresome?

*P29:* I try to find out.

K: Don't try to find out. Here is a question: Why has man — why have we — made such a mess of the world, mess of our lives, mess of other people's lives? You understand, sir? It is a mess, it is a confusion; why? Listen to the question, go into the question.

Have you ever held in your hands a marvellous jewel? You look at it, don't you? You see the intricacies of it, how beautifully it is put together, what extraordinary skill has gone into it, right? The silversmith must have had marvellous hands. The jewel is very important; you look at it, you cherish it, you put it away in the case and look at it, don't you?

*P29:* I want to have it.

K: Yes, you have it in your hand, sir; I am saying you look at it. Your marvellous picture is painted by somebody or other and you look at it. It is in your room, it is yours — you just do not hang it and forget it; you look at it. In the same way, if I ask you a question, look at it, listen to the question. But we are so quick to answer it, so impatient. So I am suggesting, sir, look at it, take time, weigh it, see the beauty of the question. It may be an utterly unimportant question. Do it, sir. Then you will find that the question itself has a tremendous energy.

*P30:* Why do we not change?

K: Why, sir? Why don't you change.

*P30:* I don't know, but I do not change.

K: Are you satisfied where you are?

*P30:* No.

K: Then change!

*P31:* Sir, I would like to ask a question, please. There is a teacher in a class in which some boy is naughty. In order to put him right, he has to punish him. Should he go through that exercise of punishment, which means violence?

K: What do you mean by the word 'violence'? Don't be quick, sir. What do you mean by violence? Hitting each other — would you call that violence? I hit you, you hit me back — that is a form of violence, isn't it? The grown-up person hits his child — that is a form of violence. Killing another is a form of violence, harassing another is a form of violence, trying to imitate another is a form of violence, right? Would you agree to that? Imitating, conforming to the pattern of another — that is violence, right? So I am asking you, how will you stop psychological violence and physical violence? Don't say people; how will *you* stop it?

*P32:* Sir, why is there variety in nature?

K: Thank god! Why do you bother about nature? Why are you concerned with nature?

*P32:* I am seeing the variety.

K: Don't you see the variety here?

*P32:* I see it even outside.

K: What are you going to do about it?

*P32:* I want to know why.

K: Sir, I would request you to study yourself first, know yourself first. You know about everything outside you, but you know nothing about yourself. This has been an old question. The Greeks have put it in their own way; the Egyptians, the ancient Hindus have said too — know yourself first. Will you start with that?

*P33:* I am always putting this question to myself: Why am I in the bondage of physical pain? I keep on asking this question, but I don't get any answer.

K: You may be going to the wrong doctor. Sir, I know people who go from doctor to doctor. They have plenty of money, so they are trotting around from one doctor to another. Do you do that, or is it psychological pain?

*P33:* Physical as well as psychological.

K: Which is important? Which is a greater pain?

*P33:* When the physical pain is extreme, surely it is the physical pain that is important.

K: Sir, you have not answered my question. To what do you give importance?

*P33:* At the moment when I am suffering, I give importance to that.

K: You have not answered my question, sir, have you? I am asking you which is more important — psychological pain or physical pain?

*P33:* What do you mean by psychological pain?

K: I will tell you. Pain of fear, pain of loneliness, pain of anxiety, pain of sorrow and so on — all that is in the psyche. Now, to what do you give importance — to the psychological or to the physical pain?

*P33:* Psychological.

K: Do you, really?

*P33:* Yes, sir.

K: Are you being obstinate, sir? If you give importance to the psychological pain, who is going to be the doctor?

*P33:* I.

K: What do you mean by 'I'? *You* are the pain. You are not different from the 'I'. The 'I' is made up of pain, anxiety, boredom, loneliness, fear, pleasure — all that is the 'I'.

*P34:* If I have understood that there is urgency to be aware all the time, how is it that I remain in that state only for a very short while during the day?

K: Because you don't understand what it means to be aware.

Sir, here is a question. It is a fact that the various centres of the KFI* constantly and continuously stress and spread that they are the centre of K's teaching. So now when we have the Buddha's teaching, Christ's teaching and Krishnamurti's teaching, are these so-called teachings of K going to meet the same fate as those of the Buddha and Christ? Have you understood the question?

Sir, K has thought a great deal about the word 'teaching'. We thought of using the word 'work' — ironworks, big building works, hydro-electric works, you understand? So I thought 'work' was very, very common. So we thought we might use the word 'teaching', but it is not important — the word — right? The teachings of the Buddha nobody knows. I have asked them about the original teachings of the Buddha, but nobody knows. And Christ may have existed or may not have existed. That is a tremendous problem, whether he existed at all. We have discussed with great scholars about

* The Krishnamurti Foundation, India.

that. I would not go into it. And will K's teachings also disappear like the rest? You understand my question?

*P35:* I have not said it.

K: Of course you have not said it; somebody has written it. Therefore it is interesting. The questioner says — probably you also think — that when K goes, as he must go, what will happen to the teaching? Will it go as the Buddha's teachings, which have been corrupted? You know what is happening; will the same fate await K's teaching? You have understood the question? It depends upon you, not upon somebody else. It depends upon you — how you limit it, how you think about it, what it means to you. If it means nothing except words, then it will go the way of the rest. If it means something very deep to you, to you personally, then it won't be corrupted. You understand? So it is up to you, not up to the centres and information centres and all the rest of that business. It depends upon you, whether you live the teachings or not.

*P36:* Has the truth its own power?

K: It has, if you let it alone.

*P37:* Sir, that question was put by me. May I clarify the question — what I mean by that?

K: Yes, sir, what is the question?

*P37:* Now, my question is this: You have so many times repeated for 70 years that you do not convince anybody of anything, you are not a teacher, you do not teach anything to anybody. Now I say that the centres of the KFI — whose president you are — they invite the public, 'Come here, here are the teachings of Krishnamurti; you study here what he has to say. He has discovered so many things. Please come here and try to study.' You say you work as a mirror; when I use the mirror, does the mirror help me?

K: Yes.

*P37:* It does help me, the light is helping me. Are these things not your teachings? So there is no harm if you say you are teaching something, you are clearing something. You yourself say that you work as a mirror; anything which works as a mirror is definitely helping me.

K: Yes, sir.

*P37:* That is my question.

K: Sir, in all his talks K has emphasized the fact that he is merely a mirror — right? — that he is merely a mirror reflecting what your life is. And he has also said you can break up that mirror if you have seen yourself very clearly; the mirror is not important. But what has happened throughout the world? They all want to be on the band-wagon. You know what that means? All want to share in the circus.

So I say, please don't bother, just listen to the teachings; if somebody wants to form a little centre in Gujarat, let him do it, but he has no power to say that he represents K, that he is a follower. He can say anything he likes, he is free to do what he likes. We are not imposing on anybody that they should do this or do that. Say, for instance, he starts by buying videos and all the rest of it and collects a few friends in his house. That is his affair. We are not saying, 'Don't do this, do that.' If anybody did that, I would say, 'Sorry, do not do it.' But they like to do it, they like to be interpreters, gurus in their little way. You know the game you all play. So if you want to do that, you are welcome to do it. The Foundation — unfortunately, I happen to belong to it, or fortunately — says you are free to do what you like — you understand, sir? Buy books, read books, burn books of K, do anything you like. It is in your hands. If you want to live it, live it; if you don't want to live it, it is all right, it is your business. Is this clear once and for all?

*P37:* Yes, sir.

K: The Foundation has no authority over your life, to tell you what to do or what not to do, or to say: 'This is the centre from which all radiation goes,' like a radio station or a television station; we are not saying that. All we are saying is: Here is something which may be original, or may not be original; here is something for you to look at. Take time to read it; take time to understand it. If you are not interested, throw it away; it does not matter. If you like to live that way, live it. If you do not, just drop it. Don't make a lot of noise around you. Do you understand what I am saying, sir? Don't make a circus of it, a song-and-dance — don't say that you have understood and will tell others all about it. Right, sir?

It is time to stop. Now, if I may ask, what have you got out of this morning's talk, discussion? Nothing or something? I am just asking, sir, what has flowered in you after this morning? Like a flower blooms overnight, what has bloomed in you? What has come out of you?

*P38:* That we should have the habit of thinking together.

K: Did you really think together?

*P38:* Yes, I did.

K: Together — you and I — or were you talking to yourself.?

*P38:* I was talking to myself also.

K: Yes. So I am just asking — you don't have to tell the speaker anything — I am just asking politely, if I may: We have met for over an hour, talked together, said many things according to our opinions; at the end of the journey this morning, where are you? — where we started, where we ended, or is there a new flowering?

I am not going to say where you are. That will be impudence on my part, right?

It is an extraordinary world, sir! You don't seem to realize it is a marvellous world, the earth — beautiful, rich, vast plains, deserts, rivers, mountains and the glory of the land. This is an unique country. But human beings are set to kill each other for the rest of their lives. If you go on like this, you will keep on repeating the pattern: killing, killing, killing. You may repeat the most marvellous poems in Sanskrit (I do too), but all that is not worth a cent if you don't live it. That is all, sir.

# RISHI VALLEY

Krishnamurti (K): May I raise a very difficult question? How would you, if you had a son here or a daughter, want to educate them, to bring about a holistic life?

You've got so many students here — capable, intelligent. Through what means, what kind of attitude, what kind of verbal explanation, would you educate them in a holistic way of living? I mean by 'holistic', whole, unbroken, not splintered up, not fragmented, as most of our lives are. So my question is, if I may put it to you, how do you bring about a holistic way of living, an outlook that's not fragmented in specializations?

*First Teacher (T1):* Sir, first we must be holistic ourselves.

K: That's understood, sir. But first of all, you are educators here, including myself (if you will permit me). I am happy in Rishi Valley, I like the place, the beauty of it, the hills, the rocks, the flowers, the shadows on the hills. I am one of the educators here; parents send me one of their children an I want to see that they live a life that is whole. Whole means good.

'Good', not in the ordinary sense of that word; not the traditional word 'good': a good boy, a good husband — that's all very limited. The word 'good' has much greater significance when you relate goodness to wholeness. Good, then, has the quality of being extraordinarily generous; good has that sense of not wanting to hurt another consciously; good, in the sense that it is correct — not only for the moment, correct all the time. Correct in the sense that it does not depend on circumstances; if it is correct now, it will be correct a hundred years later or ten days later. Correctness with goodness is not related to environment, circumstances, pressures and so on. From that comes right action. So, goodness and a holistic way of living go together. In what manner am I going to see that the boy grows in goodness and a holistic way of living? Do we rely on each other? Is it an individual problem, or is it a problem of the whole school, the whole body? So the action must be comprehensive — not that that gentleman thinks one way and I think another way about goodness; it must be a cohesive action. Now, is that possible?

Sir, in the word 'holistic' is implied not the orthodox, the organized, but that quality of religion which we will go into presently. How am I, living here as an educator, to bring this about?

*T2:* The first thing we have to do is to make the child feel secure in his relationship. It seems to me that unless the child feels secure in his relationship, with me and the place, nothing can happen.

*T3:* I want to find out whether what you say is really what I want to do. If I feel that is really what I want to do, then I must find out what I mean by that, what is the content of my feelings.

*T4:* Would it be necessary, if you and I are working together in the school, to find out, not what I mean by that or what you mean, but rather find out if there is something that is valid for all of us? Not because we stick to an idea or come together around an idea, but in the investigation we say together, 'This is it.'

K: Sir, do we understand what it means to live a holistic life? Or is it a theory?

*T3:* Sir, perhaps we merely understand by contrast. We see fragmentation in ourselves . . .

K: If you see fragmentation or breaking-up in yourself, then you have the problem of how to get rid of it, how to be whole. I don't want a problem about it. Then I have already broken it up.

*T3:* Despite that, the fact remains that we are fragmented.

K: Just a minute. I know I am fragmented; my whole thinking process is fragmented. And also I know I mustn't make a problem of it because then that's another fragmentation.

*T3:* My feeling of fragmentation is itself a problem — I don't *make* a problem; I *see* a problem.

K: I understand. I realize I am fragmented, but I don't want to make a problem of it.

*T3:* But, sir, doesn't it mean that when I see that I am fragmented, it is a problem?

K: That's what I want to get at, which is — I see I am fragmented: I say one thing and I do another, think one thing and contradict what I think. And I also see very clearly that I mustn't make a problem of it.

*T3:* Perhaps I don't see that clearly.

K: That's what I want to discuss. If I make a problem of it, I am already further fragmenting.

*T3:* But there is an in-between stage.

K: I don't want that. I am fragmented, broken up in different ways. If I make a problem of it, saying to myself, I must not be fragmented, that very statement is born out of fragmentation. Something born of fragmentation is another form of fragmentation. But my brain is trained to make problems. So I must be aware of the whole cycle of it. So what am I to do?

*T1:* You say to that, 'I should not make a problem of it.' Do we have a choice, or is it automatic? When we see the fragmentation within us, we say, 'I would not like to make a problem of it.'

K: See the *truth*, not 'I will not make a problem.' I see the fact that if I make a problem of it, it's another fragmentation. That's all. I see it. I don't say, I mustn't get rid of it or I must get rid of it, so what am I to do?

*T1:* Is there anything to be done in this case?

K: I am going to show you presently. Don't be so eager, if you don't mind my saying so.

*T1:* The way I see it, there is nothing to be done except actually watching, observing.

K: Just a minute, sir. Don't come to that conclusion. What am I to do?

*T1:* Observe.

K: Don't tell me, sir. These are words. Seeing that I am fragmented, aware that whatever I do is another kind of fragmentation, what is left for me? You don't put yourself in that position; you have already come to a conclusion. So conclusion is another fragmentation. I have this question: Is there a way of living holistically in which is involved the quality of a religious mind, deep goodness, without any mischief, without any duality? Am I making it complicated?

*T5:* No, sir.

K: Why not, sir? My whole being thinks dualistically. It's always in opposition in the sense that I want to do this, and yet I mustn't do it; I should do it, but I don't like to do it, and so on. It always takes opposing positions. So, what is left for me? I see all this at a glance, or through analysis. And I see it is like that. Then my question is: what am I to do? Don't tell me: you should or shouldn't — I don't accept anything from you; I am very sceptical by nature.

*T1:* You are asking the question: what am I to do? When there is observation, no question arises.

K: Are you doing it?

*T1:* Yes.

K: Are you doing it? If you are not doing it and you say we must try, you are in contradiction, therefore duality, therefore fragmentation, and hence no goodness.

*T6:* As soon as you say or think about a holistic state of goodness, you are already in contradiction.

K: No, you are not in contradiction. You are only putting it into words. What's your action when you want to educate your student in this goodness?

The school has a certain reputation, a certain éclat — a feeling about it. And there is a certain atmosphere in this valley. And I sent you my son, hoping that you will help him to grow in this holistic way of life. I am communicating, I am not contradicting.

*T5:* It is in the way I posit the question that the contradiction arises.

K: I understand. We are trying to investigate the question, not lay down laws about it. At least I'm not. I really want to find out what way I can help the student. I may not be holistic. Don't say: first I must be holistic, and then I can teach. Then you are dead. Then that will take an eternity. If you say: I must first be holistic, then you have stymied yourself. Sir, I am not saying *anything*. I really don't know what to do with these children whose parents want them to join the IIT* or something or other. And I've got the tremendous opposition of society — the father, the mother, the grandfather, wanting the boy to have a job and all that. How am I to bring this about? You don't answer me.

*T4:* Krishnaji, I am not answering the question how am I to bring this about; I'm looking at fragmentation.

K: What does that mean? Follow it out — I am fragmented, the boy is fragmented. Right, sir?

*T4:* Right.

K: Then what's the relationship between me and the boy?

*T4:* We are learning together.

K: Don't use phrases quickly. What's my relationship with the student who is fragmented like myself?

*T7:* I am not different from him.

K: Of course you are different from him — you teach maths, he doesn't know any. Don't say you are not different from him.

*T4:* There is no relationship at all if I am fragmented.

K: Please, sir, answer my question: I am fragmented, and I am your student. What's our relationship? Or, is there any relationship at all? Or, are we on the same level?

*T5:* It can only be a fragmented relationship.

K: What is *actually* my relationship?

*T5:* There doesn't seem to be any.

K: That's all. How can fragments have a relationship?

*T6:* Why not?

K: Are you really asking me that question?

*T6:* Yes.

* The Indian Institute of Technology.

K: *You* answer it. You ask me a question, and I am too eager to reply to it. So it goes on between you and me: I answer it and then you counter it; then I counter it, and so on. He asks me a question and he expects me to answer it, and I say: I won't answer it because in the question itself is the answer. So, can we look at the question and wait for it to flower? My question is very, very serious. The question itself contains the answer if you let it flower, if you let it alone, not cover it immediately with a response. Your response is already conditioned, already personal. So leave the question. If the question has depth, significance, vitality, then the question unfolds.

Now, sir, is there truth? Does truth exist? You don't know, if you're honest; so we leave the question. Let's look at the question, and the question begins to unfold: Is there truth, or only active, vital, illusion? I won't go into that. If the question has depth, if the question has a sense of great vitality — because you are asking the question in great inward searching — let the question answer itself. It will if you leave it alone.

Now I am coming back to my original question.

*T8:* I have a child come to me. I am fragmented, he is fragmented. So there is no relationship?

K: Are you sure there is no relationship, or are you just saying it?

*T8:* I think I am sure there is no relationship in the fragmented state, and I find that any response that I give to the student would itself be a fragmented response.

K: Yes. Stop there. Then, what will you do? Whatever relationship I have is still fragmented. Is that a reality or a verbal statement?

*T8:* It seems a reality to me.

K: Either it is real in the sense that the microphone is real; that's not an illusion. The *word* microphone is not *that*. I don't know if you get the quality of it.

So we must come back. What am I to do, sir? *You* tell me.

*T8:* Am I fooling myself that I can give a holistic education?

K: We are going to find out, you and I, whether it is possible to do it or not. The first statement is: we are fragmented. Let's stick to that. We are both fragmented, and I don't know what to do. What does that mean to you — I don't know; I don't know what to do? Then, I must investigate. When I *say*, I don't know, I really *mean* I don't know. Or, am I waiting for somebody else to tell me, so I will know? Which is it?

*T8:* At the moment the latter.

K: Is there a state of the brain when it says: I really don't know? I am not waiting for him to answer, or expecting someone else to tell me. All these are states when I am waiting for an answer. But no one can answer this because they are all fragmented. Therefore I am waiting, watching, looking, observing, listening to the question. I don't know what to do. Then I ask myself, 'What's the state of my brain which says: "I don't know"?'

*T5:* At that point of time, it's not functioning.

K: 'I don't know'. Or are you waiting for it to know?

*T5:* Waiting for it to know.

K: Therefore, you are waiting to know; you *will* know. Therefore your brain is not saying, 'I don't know.' It's all very logical, you know.

*T3:* The brain doesn't say it doesn't know.

K: That's it, that's the first thing — the brain never acknowledges or remains in the state 'I don't know'. You ask me: 'What is Ishvara?' and I promptly answer. You have read, or you believe or you don't believe; Ishvara comes as a symbol to you. But if you ask, 'What is the element which created this?' it's a tremendously interesting question: What is the beginning of life? What is the life in the seed that you plant? The life of man — what is the origin of that life, the very cell? I am not going into this now — it leads off somewhere else, it's too complicated.

So I don't know how to deal with that boy or with myself. Any action I do, any movement of thought, is still out of fragmentation, right? So I leave it alone. May I proceed?

*T6:* Please, sir.

K: What is love? Is it related to hate? If it is related, love then is still fragmentation. Do you understand what I am saying, sir?

*T6:* Love is not the opposite of hate.

K: What is love? It has nothing to do with pity, sympathy — all the rest of it. What is love? You don't know. Is that state of not-knowing love?

I don't know what to do with that boy or girl; we are both fragmented. I can teach him mathematics, geography, history, biology, chemistry, psychiatry, anything — but that's nothing. This demands much deeper enquiry, very much deeper. So I say, what is it that is completely holistic? Certainly not thought — thought is experience. It's certainly not sympathy, not generosity, not empathy, not saying: 'You're a nice chap.' Love has — what?

*T5:* Compassion.

K: Love, compassion — that is the only thing that's holistic. I'm just discovering something for myself. I say, love isn't thought, love isn't pleasure. Don't accept this; for god's sake that is the last thing you should do. Love is utterly unrelated

to hate, jealousy, anger — all that. Love is completely
unbreakable. It's whole and it has its own intelligence.

*T5:* I have heard you say this before in different ways.

K: To know. Can you ever say about a person — 'I know'? I
know my wife?

*T3:* You shut off that person in some way.

K: Yes. If I say, 'I know you' — what do I know about you?
So, to say 'I know' is fragmentation.

Sir, I asked a question, which is: can I help the student or
talk to him? I know I am fragmented, he is fragmented. And
I also know, have a feeling, that love is whole, that
compassion, love, have their own intelligence. I am going to
see if that intelligence can operate.

*T6:* You say that love has its own intelligence; you say that
love is holistic, it's not fragmented. Isn't that just an
assumption?

K: It's not an assumption. Love is not an assumption — my
god!

*T6:* Maybe it is, because I don't know.

K: Remain there. You don't know. Wait, find out; don't
answer. I don't know what the insides of a modern car are
like. (I have, as a matter of fact, stripped old cars.) So I want
to learn about it. I go to a garage man and he teaches me
because I want to know how it works. I take the trouble; I
take pains; I pay him, if I have the money, or work with him
till I know every part of that car. That means I wish to learn,
but I'm not sure *you* want to learn.

*T2:* But Krishnaji, this very wanting to learn . . .

K: Don't translate into fragmentation.

I don't know how those cameras work, and you say, learn about it. I ask him, and I become his apprentice; I watch how he does it; I learn about it. Then I say: I know how to work that camera. But human beings are not like cameras; they are much more complicated. They are like a messy machine; and I want to know how their brain works. Either I become a biologist, a brain specialist, or I study myself, which is much more exciting. So I learn how my brain works — there is nobody to teach me.

*T2:* There may be — I listen to you.

K: I don't trust them. All their knowledge is from books or from their little selves. So I say, I am going to investigate this whole way of living, not just parts of it.

So let's come back: what am I to do or not do? The question is much deeper than merely the boy and the girl whom I'm educating. It might be that I have not really understood what it means to lead a holistic life; not understood intellectually even.

*T2:* If you mean intellectually, I would say yes.

K: No, no, no. Are you sure?

*T2:* I'm sure — intellectually.

K: So you have separated the intellect from the whole. Sir, listen; when you say you have understood intellectually, it means just bananas.

*T2:* I don't just *say*; I've *understood* intellectually.

K: I say, sir, you are not listening. When one says, I understood intellectually, it means absolutely nothing; when you say 'intellectually', that's another fragment.

*T2:* Yes, sir.

K: So, I don't use the words: 'I understand intellectually.' That's a crime! What am I, an educator at Rishi Valley, understanding partially, verbally, a holistic way of living, and knowing that the student and I are both fragmented — what am I going to do or not do? Are you listening?

I'm here, I'm responsible to the parents for that girl or boy. They have sent them here because you have a good reputation, you look after them and all that. He comes along and tells me: It's all right, but what matters is a holistic way of life, not intellectually but the whole psyche, the whole entity which is now fragmented; if that can be made whole, then you have the most extraordinary education. He tells me that and he goes away, and I don't know what to do. I understand the verbal meaning of *whole*: not fragmented, not broken up, not saying one thing, thinking something and doing quite the opposite — all that is fragmentation of life. And I don't know what to do; I really don't. Deeply, profoundly, gravely, seriously, I don't know what to do. Am I waiting for somebody or some book to tell me, or hoping something will accidentally come along and give me, unfortunately, 'insight'? I can't wait for that, because the boy is growing up and kicking around.

So, what shall I do? I know one thing absolutely for certain: *I don't know*. All my inventions, all my thinking have collapsed. I don't know whether you feel that way. *I don't know* — so the brain is open for reception. The brain has been closed by conclusion, by opinion, by judgement, by my problems; it is a closed thing. When I say, *I really don't know*, I've broken something; I've broken the bottle — I can drink the champagne.

I begin to find out — when the bottle is broken. Then I find out what love is, what compassion is, and that intelligence that's born of compassion. It's nothing to do with the intellect.

Sir, we never come to the point when we say: I don't know. Right? You ask me about god, I've an immediate answer.

You ask me about chemistry, out comes the answer — the tap is open.

You see, I'm one of those idiots, sir; haven't read a thing, except . . .

*T2:* And doesn't think also.

K: The brain is like a drum; it's all tuned up. When you strike it, it gives the right note.

# RISHI VALLEY

*First Teacher (T1):* Is a new mind the same as a good mind, a mind that is flowering in goodness? If so, what is goodness? And, in particular, what is the relationship of a new mind to an awareness of the wholeness of life? What is the whole of life? Can we explore this in some depth?

KRISHNAMURTI (K): I wonder how you regard life. What do you consider is the origin of life, the beginning of all existence? Not only of human beings, but also the whole world, nature, the heavens and the stars? What is creation?

We are not asking what invention is. Invention is based on knowledge. Inventing more and more, is naturally based on knowledge. And what is our life in relation to the whole of it? Not in relation to a particular specialized brain but in relation to the whole world which is a total movement, including ourselves, including humanity?

I would like to discuss that with you first. Then, is there a difference between our physical brain — the biological thing which is inside the skull — and the mind? Or does the brain contain the mind, or is the mind totally different from the brain?

And the third question, or movement — I would prefer it to be a movement, not a question — What would you call goodness, the flowering in goodness? Not static goodness, but a movement in goodness?

*T1:* What is life?

K: Yes, what is life? Not life in a particularised form like the ape, the tiger, the squirrel, the tree, all that. What is the beginning of life?

And the other question is: Does the brain contain the mind, or is the mind totally divorced from the brain? If the brain contains the mind, then the mind is part of matter — right? — part of the nervous responses. It is a physical phenomenon. And the mind surely is something totally different.

So, if the brain includes the mind, then it is part of our nervous, biological reactions of fear, sorrow, pain, pleasure, the total consciousness. Then it is part of human creation. If the mind is part of an evolutionary process, then it is part of time.

*T2:* May I ask a question?

K: Sir, you don't have to ask me.

*T2:* Through logic, suppose we find that the mind is different from the brain; and logic itself is part of the brain?

K: Of course logic is part of the brain, and logic can come to a wrong conclusion because it is still part of the brain.

So, what is life? What is the source of all this energy? What is the thing that shoots out, making all this — the world, the earth, the mountains, the rivers, the forests, the trees, the bear, the deer, the lion, the ape, the monkey, and us?

Is time involved in goodness? If time is involved in goodness, it is not goodness. Please answer me. Do you understand my question?

*T3:* Sir, there doesn't seem at the moment to be a connection between the two. When the scientists talk of the origin of things, I believe, the generally accepted theory is that there was the big bang, an enormous explosion, stemming perhaps from some primal energy, stemming perhaps from some infinitesimal atom. And after this came the whole multiplicity of things, the stars, the planets, the earth. There doesn't seem, at first sight, to be any connection between that scientific explanation and goodness.

K: I am asking, sir, is time involved in goodness?

*T3:* Time is certainly involved in the evolution of things. That is obvious.

K: Is goodness part of time, cultivated or brought about through time?

*T3:* It doesn't seem, if one looks at the scientific view of the origin of things, as if goodness is involved in that at all. It seems completely neutral — not good, not bad, not anything.

K: I understand that, but I am asking you a question — not a scientific question. The question is: If time is involved in the cultivation of goodness, is that goodness at all?

*T3:* Seems to be a different order of question.

K: I am asking you a different question. What is goodness? What do you all think is goodness?

*T3:* There seems to be a version of goodness which is usually opposed to badness or evil . . .

K: Yes, the whole duality business. Go on, sir. What is goodness here? What do you think is goodness?

*T4:* Virtue can be practised in time.

K: I am not talking about virtue. To me virtue is a cultivation.

*T5:* Sir, when we say he is a good man, we generally mean that he doesn't harm others. He doesn't act always out of self-interest, gain . . . It is a quality accumulated in time.

K: Is it? Is goodness the opposite of badness — if such a word exists? Is good the opposite of bad?

*T5:* Sir, what you mean by this question is, is goodness a reaction to the bad and accumulated over time?

K: Yes, all that is implied in the question. One's reaction, one's education, one's culture, environment; all that is tradition — what you read in books and so on. Always the good and the bad. The good fighting the bad, always, from the ancient Egyptians to modern society. There was always the good and the bad, the good god and the bad god, the bad guy and the good guy.

I am saying, if I may, that if the good is born out of the bad, then it is not good.

*T3:* It is usually looked at the other way round — that the evil is a fall from the good.

K: Sir, I am asking you, is the good related to the bad? Is good the opposite of bad or the reaction which had become the good? Do you understand my question? Or has good nothing to do with, is totally divorced from, bad?

*T5:* Sir, while I would be able to answer the first question, I am not able to answer the second. The first question being, is the good related to the bad? I would say no, because if I try to be good, then automatically the bad continues.

K: Sir, are you saying that the ideas of the whole evolutionary process of the good and the bad, from the most ancient times, are totally mistaken? That's what we are saying. Do you understand? Come on, sir.

*T5:* Yes. That's the implication.

K: That the good cannot fight the evil. Right? And throughout the history of man, good is always fighting evil. Great paintings, great art, the whole of human existence is based on this principle. And you and I come along and say, 'Look, there is something wrong with this. Good is totally different from bad; there is no relationship between them; therefore they cannot fight. Good cannot overcome evil.'

*T3:* There is no progression either.

K: Are we saying something totally revolutionary? Or is it some sort of fantasy or imagination of ours?

*T6:* One of the problems we face is that we have grown used to using particular words in a particular way.

K: Our whole religious conditioning, our whole religious literature, is full of it. There is always hell and heaven, good and bad.

So are we saying something totally revolutionary? And is it true? Something revolutionary may not be true. If it is true, it has nothing to do with the brain.

*T1:* The implication seems to be that goodness exists prior to man. It seems to mean that goodness is inherent in the universe.

K: Maybe.

*T1:* It seems to mean that.

K: We are asking the question in relation to what is the brain. What is the mind? Can the mind penetrate the brain?

*T1:* Again this will imply that the mind is prior to the brain.

K: Of course. Let us call that 'intelligence' for the moment. Can that intelligence communicate through the brain? Or can the brain not have any relationship with that intelligence?

*T7:* Is the brain born of that intelligence?

K: I'm not prepared yet for that question. I am asking you the question. Don't listen to me, sir. I'm not telling you; you and I are enquiring.

*T1:* I don't want an answer.

K: Are you finding out for yourself? Or are you listening to the man? Or is what the speaker says clearing a way for you to see?

*T1:* This question seems to direct our attention to the universe. Or to nature.

K: That's what we want to get at. Slowly. Is the universe — our idea of the universe — different from us? It's all one movement — the stars, the heavens, the moon, the sun; one tremendous energy. Our energy is very limited. Can that limitation be broken down and we be part of that enormous movement of life?

*T1:* Would you call this enormous movement 'nature'?

K: No, I wouldn't call it nature. Nature is part of us.

*T1:* This total movement.

K: Is there such a movement? Not 'I join the movement' because I am such a small speck. I think I can be very clever; I think I can do this, do that. Can all that be broken down and be part of this enormous movement? I call this goodness. I may be wrong. The window which is so narrow now must be broken down, and then — no window at all. I don't know if I am expressing myself.

What then is life? Is it that immense intelligence which is energy, supreme, unconditioned, uneducated — in the sense of the modern term — something that has no beginning and no end?

*T5:* Are you implying that creation does not involve time?

K: Invention involves time. Now they are trying to find a cure for cancer. All the books, magazines talk about new methods, to cure cancer. The discovery involves time and knowledge, built on what the previous person has discovered. I learn from you, you learn from him. Creation cannot involve time. I don't know if you see.

*T8:* When you are talking about time, you mean psychological time.

K: Of course, psychological time.

So goodness is not involved in time, therefore it is part of that intelligence which is universal movement. I'm using words I may withdraw later.

Here I am then with a thousand students. As a good educator, I want to see that they understand all this. Not intellectually, not theoretically, not as some fantastic idea, but so that there is real transformation — no, not transformation — so that a real mutation takes place in their lives.

*T1:* When you say 'immense intelligence', the word 'intelligence' implies some quality of awareness.

K: It may not.

*T1:* But then, what is the quality that is intelligent?

K: Probably it has no quality. It is intelligence. You see what you are doing. You are giving it a virtue, a significance, so that you can understand it. I may not be capable of understanding it. I don't know. You see, it may be something incredible or it may be nothing at all. I can't approach this with a mind that says, show me your qualifications, show me your degree.

So what am I to do after an educational conference? What am I to do, as an educator, to bring about a mutation? Not a transformation; there is a difference. Transformation means from one to another, from this to that.

*T9:* Sir, can we come back to something we skipped over some time ago? We talked about the ending of the limitation we are trapped in; that ending and something else happening. Can we go back to that? For there seems to be something in that we quickly skipped over.

K: My brain has been educated, has lived in tradition, whether ancient or modern tradition, my brain has been mauled about, informed, beaten, by all the conditioning that has gone on for centuries. Can that be broken down? Is that your question? Are you sure?

T9: Yes. All of those things that make it possible for this brain to have any relationship with goodness.

K: Let's break it down to one word: consciousness. Can we?

T9: Yes.

K: Or 'limitation' or 'conditioning'. Can all that be broken down? Not through time — that is important. If I use time, I am back in the circle. Do you see that?

T9: Yes, sir.

K: So it must be broken down. Instantly. Not in comparison to, or in relation to, time.

T10: Again, you mean psychological time.

K: Yes, of course. Psychological time is different from ordinary time. I don't know if you see that. Do you? Time by that clock, time by the sun, time to cover a physical distance. We don't know each other, but if we meet often, we will. Or we may know each other instantly. So there is physical time and psychological time. We are talking of psychological time. It takes time for a seed to grow, for a child to become a man. We apply that kind of time to the psyche. I am this, but I will be that; I am not brave, but give me time and I will be. We are talking of time in the field of the psyche.

T1: Can the limitation of consciousness be broken?

K: That is the question. Can the limited brain — which is knowledge — break down the whole field of the psyche? Can the brain break it down — the limited brain? However much it has evolved, this brain will always be limited.

*T1:* By it's knowledge.

K: It is limited by its physical structure, by its very physical environment, by its tradition, education, knowledge, pain, fear, anxiety. Can that limitation break itself down?

*T9:* Or, can anything else break it down?

K: Wait, sir. Stick to the one question. Can the limited brain break down its own limitation?

*T8:* Sir, you said good is not related to bad.

K: Don't begin all that. Let's stick to the one question: Can the smallness of the brain break down its own pettiness? Or is there another factor that will break it down? God? Saviour? Vishnu? It can invent god and wait for him to clear it up. Do I make myself clear? Both of you have put that question. After putting that question, what is the state of your brain? After putting that question, what has happened to your brain? The question is important, has weight, has great significance. Tell me, what is the state of your brain after putting that question? It is very important to find out.

*T11:* It is not depending on god. It is not sure.

K: Are you listening? You have been asking a question. It may be very important, or it may not have any meaning at all. So, I am asking myself: What is the state of your brain after putting that question?

*T11:* After listening to the question — 'Can the petty brain break down its own pettiness?' — what first arose in my brain was: I doubt it, I doubt whether the petty brain can break down its pettiness.

K: Your brain is acting.

*T11:* Then it said, 'I don't know.'

K: But you are still saying something. Your brain is still active, saying, 'I don't know, I'm waiting.'

*T₁₁:* Sir, why did you use the words, 'You are waiting?'

K: Don't bother. Your brain is active. So what is happening? Just watch, sir. One of them puts this question to me. How do I receive this question? How do I interpret the question? If I interpret the question, I'm not listening to it. So, am I actually listening to the question? Or, as the question is put, do I immediately respond to something, in which case I am not listening at all? It's a verbal communication and I pass it by.

So, do I listen? That implies a certain quality of quietness — a thoughtless movement, a thoughtless looking. What is the state of your brain when a serious question is put? If your brain is at all active, then the question has no meaning. Am I making myself clear?

Someone puts that question to me. What is important is how I receive it, not the answer. I listen very carefully. The question is, 'Can the narrow, conditioned brain break down its conditioning?' I'm listening to the question. I'm still listening to the question. Am I actually listening or just saying I'm listening? If I'm actually listening, then there is no movement in the brain at all. Of course, there is a nervous response — hearing through the ear, etc. But, apart from the verbal communication, there is no other movement. I'm still listening — that is the breaking down. I don't know if you know what I'm talking about.

*T₁:* Because the brain is not acting.

K: Don't translate it. I don't know if I am making myself clear — that the very state of listening is the state of ending of a certain thing.

So, is that happening? If that is happening to you, then how am I, as an educator, to make those students, for whom I'm responsible, listen? How am I to help them to listen to what I have to say?

*T6:* There is a difficulty here. When you explain something in person, it seems clear. But tomorrow morning . . .

K: Then you haven't heard. You've heard the hiss of a cobra, haven't you? I used to hear them very often when I walked alone here. I used to see them. And I know a cobra now. Even tomorrow, I will know a cobra. That is an actual fact. Right? Here some kind of sensitivity, watchfulness, alertness is needed.

How am I, as an educator, having heard all this, having absorbed it in my blood — it's not as if I just heard you, therefore I learnt it, it's not just that — but after having heard all that, how am I to see that the students listen to me? You make them listen to you in mathematics, learning a book, biology, history, etc.

Suppose I come to a class and I say, 'Please sit down and listen.' They're looking out of the window, they are pulling each other's hair. In that state of mind, can they listen? Or, do I say, 'Keep quiet for ten minutes'? But these ten minutes are gone in battling; the brain saying, 'I must listen, who the hell is he, asking me to listen?' And all the rest of it. So, how do I cajole, bring round these students to listen?

Sir, how do you make your — I was going to say 'victims' — listen to you? How does a doctor or a psychiatrist make a patient listen to him? The patient is all the time concerned about getting cured. He has a particular disease, mania, etc., he wants to be free of it. Tell him what to do and he will do it. Here it is not like that. We are all equals; there is no doctor, nobody to tell you. We are in a state of listening, of enquiry. How do we persuade one person to listen to another? Answer the question.

*T5:* Either of the two ways, sir. Either I entertain him, or I force him.

K: Yes. I don't want to do either — force, fight, or beat him up.

*T5:* Or entertain?

K: It is all the same. I want them to listen, so that it is all part of their blood. So, how do we proceed, sir?

*T8:* Must I not listen to them? To what they have to say?

K: They have very little to say, sir. They're quarrelling, muttering, saying, 'Give me this, that,' etc.

So, I am asking you as educators, 'How do I bring them round to actually listening to what I have to say?' See how long it has taken us to listen to each other. You are willing to listen, to find out. You think K has something to say, we have invited him here. Therefore, there is communication already taking place. But with those students it is different. They are forced to come here, their parents praise Rishi Valley. They come after swallowing the bitter pill, coated with sugar, of course. And so this goes on. Here, with you, it is different. You don't want to do a thing to persuade them. It is marvellous. Put that question to yourself and see what you can do.

*T9:* Sir, I think it is obvious that we cannot answer this question; and yet this seems to be central to all that we mean to do. That actually is quite a good summary of the conference.

K: I understand what you are saying.

*T1:* Perhaps here we come back to the beginning — that it requires an action which is creative.

K: Now you've said it. Leave it there. Work it out. That creativity is not born of knowledge or previous experience. Keep that in mind. If it makes use of knowledge, then it becomes invention, just a new way of doing the same thing.

We are asking a very, very serious question. I think it may be that we are all so terribly informed — about everything. Maybe we are so educated that there is no space for anything new to take place; full of memories, remembrances. All that may be a hindrance. Now, don't ask, 'How am I to get rid of it?' Then we come back to the same thing.

Suppose you tell me I'm a liar. And I give you all the reasons why I've lied — which is another lie. I hear the word 'lie' and I react. I think I'm an honest man. I may not be, but I think I am. Those are two different things. Or, I think I am a truthful man and an incident takes place which makes me untruthful. That instant of discovery — seeing I'm a liar — changes everything. That is my point. It changes me so that I'm no longer dishonest. I've experimented with this. So it is possible. No, I can't even say that.

Can I listen to you when you tell me I'm a liar and not bring up all the reasons? In that act of listening, there is a breakdown.

*T3:* Surely if the statement is true, there is a breakdown. If I'm not a liar, then there isn't.

K: No, sir. The word 'lie' is good enough for me. You understand? I know the reasons why I've lied: a little bit of cowardice. I lied because I don't want them to discover this or that. And when you call me a liar, then I see the actual fact that it is so. I don't go into all the reasons why I've lied. And you tell me, 'You are that.' And I listen to you without saying whether you are right or wrong, not putting up a barrier. In that very instant when I am listening without barriers, the thing goes. Something happens. That is the only action, which is inaction.

*T3:* But the statement itself may be false.

K: May be false. But good enough for me to see that there is some truth in it.

Now, where are we after four days? Are we together? What have you absorbed? And is that absorption common to us all, or are we trying to unify all the schools — being but parts —

trying to put them together? Which means that they will always be apart. Or is there a feeling that we are all one, so that our education is not based on American, Indian or English conditions?

So, are we merely a body to supply demands? Or are we to bring about a different human quality, a different human activity of the brain? Are we united in that? Are we together in this? Are we together so that nothing can break us apart? From that, an action which is totally different can take place.

# MADRAS

ON A WEEK-DAY, to see so many people seems rather absurd, doesn't it? Last time we met here — it was Saturday — we talked about what is love. You may remember if you were here. We are going to enquire together — and I mean together — into this whole problem; it's very, very complex. If you don't mind, you have to think — not just agree; you have to exercise your brain, thinking it out. So we are going to enquire together into this problem of what is love. *Together.* You and I are walking up the same street; you are not just following the speaker; you are not saying: 'Yes, this sounds good; so do the Upanishads and so does the Geeta,' and all that bilge.

First of all, one has to doubt, be sceptical of your experiences, conclusions, thoughts. Doubt. Question — not accepting a thing from any book, including mine; I'm a passer by, not important. And we are going to enquire together to see what is clear, and what is not clear. We are together examining, doubting, never accepting what the speaker has to say. This is not a lecture to guide, to instruct, to help; that would be too stupid. We've had that kind of help for generations upon generations and we are what we are now.

We must start from what we are now, not what we have been in the past or what we will be in the future. What we shall be in the future is what we are now. Our greed, our envy, our jealousy, our great superstitions, our desire to worship somebody — this is what we are now.

So we are together walking up a very long street — it requires energy — and we are going to go into this question: What is love? To enquire very deeply, very profoundly into it, we must also enquire: What is energy? Every gesture you make is based on energy. While you are listening to the speaker, you are exercising energy. To build a house, to plant a tree, to make a gesture, to talk, all these require energy. The crow calling, the rising and setting sun, all this is energy. The cry of the baby out of the womb is part of energy. To play a violin, to speak, to marry, have sex — everything on earth requires energy.

So we start: what is energy? This is one of the questions of the scientists. And they say: Energy is matter. It may be matter, but previous to that, what is primordial energy? What is its origin, the source? Who created this energy? Careful. Don't say 'god', and run away with that. I don't accept god; the speaker has no god. Is that all right?

So what is energy? We are enquiring, not accepting what the scientists have to say. And, if you can, abandon all that the ancient peoples have said; leave it at the roadside. We'll take a journey together.

Your brain, which is matter, is the accumulated experience of a million years, and all that evolution means energy. And so I'm asking myself — you're asking yourself — is there an energy which is not contained or stimulated or held within the field of knowledge, that is, within the field of thought? Is there an energy which is not put together by thought?

Thought gives you great energy: to go to the office every morning at nine o'clock; to earn money, a better house. Thinking about the past, thinking about the future, planning for the present, gives tremendous energy: you work like blazes to become a rich man. Thought creates this energy. So then we have to enquire into the very nature of thought.

Thought has planned this society which has divided this world into communist, socialist, democrat, republican; the army, the navy, the air-force — not only for transportation, but also to kill. So thought is very important in our lives because without thought we can't do anything; everything is contained in the process of thought.

So what is thinking? You work it out, don't listen to me. The speaker has talked about this a lot, so don't go back to my books, don't say, I've heard all this before. Here you forget all the books, all the things you have read, for we must approach this each time anew.

Thinking is based on knowledge. And we have accumulated tremendous knowledge: how to sell each other, how to exploit each other, how to create gods and temples, and so on.

Without experience there is no knowledge. Experience — knowledge stored in the brain as memory — is the beginning of thought. Experience is always limited, because you are adding more and more to it. So experience is limited, knowledge is limited, memory is limited. Therefore, thought is limited. The gods whom thought has created — your gods, your thinking — will always be limited. And from this limitation we try to find the source of energy — you understand? — we try to find the origin, the beginning of creation.

Thought has created fear. Right? Aren't you frightened of what may happen later — losing your job, not passing your exams, not climbing the ladder? And you're frightened of not being able to fulfil, of not being able to stand alone, of not being a strength unto yourself. You always depend on somebody, and that breeds tremendous fear.

It's one of the daily facts of our life that we are frightened people. And fear arises because we want security. Fear destroys love; love cannot exist where fear is. Fear on its own is a tremendous energy. And love has no relationship to fear; they're totally divorced.

So, what is the origin of fear? To question all this is to be alive, to understand the nature of love. Thinking has created fear — thinking about the future, the past, of not being able to adjust quickly to the environment, what might happen: my wife might leave me or might die; I'll be a lonely man; what will I do then? I have several children; so I had better remarry someone or other; at least she'll look after my children — and so on. This is thinking of the future, based upon the past. So thinking and time are involved in this — thinking about the future, the future being tomorrow. And thinking about that causes fear. And so time and thought are the central factors of fear.

So time and thought are the principal factors of life. Time is both inward — I am this, I will be that — and outward. And time is thought; they are both movements.

Then what place have death, pain, anxiety, suffering, loneliness, despair, all those terrible things I've gone through? — All the travail that man goes through — is that all our life? I'm asking you: Is this all your life?

This is your life. Your consciousness, if you examine it very carefully, is made up of its content: what you think, your tradition, your education, your knowledge, your time, your fears, your loneliness. That is what you are. It's a fact that your suffering, your pain, your anxiety, your loneliness, your knowledge, are shared by every human being. Every human being on this earth goes through sorrow, pain, anxiety, quarrels, coaxing, wanting this, not wanting this. So you are not an individual; you are not a separate soul, a separate *atman*. Your consciousness, which is what you are — not physically, but psychologically, inwardly — is the consciousness of mankind.

We are trying to find out, to enquire into, what is life. We're saying that as long as there is fear of any kind, the other cannot exist. If there is attachment of any kind, the other cannot exist — the other being love.

So we are going to see what the world is and enquire into
what is death. Why are we all so frightened of death? You
know what it means to die; haven't you seen dozens of people
killed, or hurt? Have you ever enquired very deeply into
what is death? It's a very important question, as important
as what is life. We said life is all this rot — knowledge, going
to the office every day at nine o'clock, etc., battling, not
wanting this, wanting that. We know what living is, but we
have never enquired seriously into what is dying.

What is dying? It must be an extraordinary thing to die.
Everything is taken away from you: your attachments, your
money, your wife, your children, your country, your superstitions, your gurus, your gods. You may wish to take them
into the other world, but you can't. So death says, 'Be totally
detached.' That's what happens when death comes: you
have no person to lean on. *Nothing.* You can believe that you
will be reincarnated. That's a very comfortable idea, but it's
not a fact.

We are trying to find out what it means to die, while living
— not committing suicide; I am not talking about that kind
of nonsense. I want to find out for myself what it means to
die, which means, can I be totally free from everything that
man has created, including myself?

What does it mean to die? To give up everything. Death
cuts you off with a very, very, very sharp razor from your
attachments, from your gods, from your superstitions, from
your desire for comfort — next life and so on. I am going to
find out what death means because it is as important as
living. So how can I find out, actually, not theoretically,
what it means to die? I actually want to find out, as you want
to find out. I am speaking for you, so don't go to sleep. What
does it mean to die? Put that question to yourself. While we
are young, or when we are very old, this question is always
there. It means to be totally free, to be totally unattached to
everything that man has put together, or what you have put

together — totally free. No attachments, no gods, no future, no past. You don't see the beauty of it, the greatness of it, the extraordinary strength of it — while living to be dying. You understand what that means? While you are living, every moment you are dying, so that throughout life you are not attached to *anything*. That is what death means.

So living is dying. You understand? Living means that every day you are abandoning everything that you are attached to. Can you do this? A very simple fact, but it has got tremendous implications. So that each day is a new day. Each day you are dying and incarnating. There is tremendous vitality, energy there because there is nothing you are afraid of. There is nothing that can hurt. Being hurt doesn't exist.

All the things that man has put together have to be totally abandoned. That's what it means to die. So can you do it? Will you try it? Will you experiment with it? Not for just a day; every day. No, sir, you can't do it; your brains are not trained for this. Your brains have been conditioned so heavily, by your education, by your tradition, by your books, by your professors. It requires finding out what love is. Love and death go together. Death says be free, nonattached, you can carry nothing with you. And love says, love says — there is no word for it. Love can exist only when there is freedom, not from your wife, from a new girl, or a new husband, but the feeling, the enormous strength, the vitality, the energy of complete freedom.

# MADRAS

TALK

*4 January 1986*

WILL YOU KINDLY participate in what he's talking about? Will you not only follow it, but together participate in it, not just think about it or casually pay attention to it? One or two things must be made very clear. This is not a personality cult. The speaker has an abomination of all that; everything he is saying is contradicted if you personally worship an individual, or make him into a god. What is important is to listen to what he has to say, share it; not only listen, but actually participate in what he's saying.

We have talked about life, the very complexity of life, the beginning of life. What is life? What is the origin of all this — the marvellous earth, the lovely evening and the early morning sun, the rivers, the valleys, the mountains and the glory of the land which is being despoiled? If you say the origin of all this is 'god', then it's finished; then you can trot along quite happily because you've solved the problem. But if you begin to question, doubt, as one should, all gods, all gurus — I don't belong to that tribe — if you begin to question all that man has put together through a long evolution down the corridors of history, you find this question asked: What is the beginning? What is the origin? How has all this come about? I hope you're asking this question; don't just listen to the speaker, but share it, tear it to pieces. Don't please, accept anything he says. He's not your guru; he's not your leader; he's not your helper. This is the platform, that is the beginning of this talk.

This is a very serious talk, and unless your brain is

actually active, one is afraid that you won't be able to follow. It would be useless for you and for the speaker to listen to a lot of words, but if we could together take a very long journey, not in terms of time, not in terms of belief or conclusions or theories, but examine very carefully the way of our lives, fear, uncertainty, insecurity and all the inventions that man has made, including the extraordinary computers — where are we at the end of two million years? Where are we going, not as some theory, not what some wretched book says, however holy it is, but where are we all going? And where have we begun? They're both related to each other: where are we going, where we began. The beginning may be the ending. Don't agree. Find out. There may be no beginning and no ending, and we're going to investigate into that together.

From the beginning of time, right down to the present day, man has always thought in terms of religion. What is religion? Man has always sought something more than this world. Men have worshipped the stars, the suns, the moons and their own creations; there has been tremendous endeavour, effort, energy, spent on ancient temples, mosques and the churches, of course. They have spent tremendous energy on this. What is the spirit of man that has sought something beyond the world, beyond the daily agony; the travail, work, going to the factory, to the office, and climbing the ladder of success, making money, trying to impress people, trying to command? Are you agreeing to this? It is a fact whether you agree or not. They're all seeking power in some form; they want to be at the centre of things — in Delhi, or here, or in other places. They want to be there.

We're asking: What is religion; what has made man give enormous treasures to a temple; what made him do all this? What was the energy that was given to all this? Was it fear? Was it seeking a reward from heaven, or whatever you like to call it? Was seeking a reward the origin? You want a reward;

you want something in exchange; you pray three or five times a day and you hope in return that some entity will give you something, from a refrigerator to a car to a better wife, or better husband, or you wait for grace, something that you can hope for, cling to. This has been the history of all religions. God and money are always together; the Catholic Church has tremendous treasures. You have it here, too, in your various temples, puja and worship and all that triviality; all that is really nonsense. We are trying to find out by enquiring very, very deeply what religion is; it is obviously not all this money-making stuff. We are asking: What is that which is nameless, which is the supreme intelligence, which has no relationship with all our prayers, with all our gods, temples, mosques, churches? That's all man-made. Any intelligent man must put all that aside and not become cynical, not become merely sceptical, but have a brain that's really active, a brain that enquires into every-thing, not only the outside world. Have we got a brain that is enquiring into its own thoughts, into its own consciousness, into its own pains, sufferings, all the rest of it? Have we got such a brain?

Here, we must separate the brain from the mind. The brain is the centre of all our nerves, our knowledge, all our theories, opinions, prejudices; from college, university, all that knowledge is gathered in the skull. All the thoughts, all the fears are there. Is the brain different from the mind? If you seriously pay attention to what the speaker has asked, is there a difference between the brain, your brain, what is inside the skull with all the knowledge you have gathered, not only you, but your forefathers and so on, for two million years, which is all encased in there — is there a difference between that brain and the mind? The brain will always be limited. Don't agree; this is much too serious. And is the mind different from this, from my consciousness, from my daily activities, from my fears, anxieties, uncertainties, sorrow, pain and all the theories which man has gathered about everything? The mind has no relationship with the brain; it can communicate with the brain, but the brain cannot communicate with it. Don't agree, please, that's the last thing to do. The speaker is saying the brain is the keeper of all our consciousness, of our thoughts, of our fears, and so on, and on, and on. All the gods, all the theories about gods and the unbelievers, it's all there. Nobody can dispute that unless he's a little bit odd. This brain, which is conditioned by knowledge, by experience, by tradition, cannot have any communication with the mind which is totally outside the activity of the brain. That mind can communicate with the brain, but the brain cannot communicate with it because the brain can imagine infinitely; the brain can imagine the nameless; the brain can do anything. The mind is too immense because it doesn't belong to you; it's not your mind.

We are going to investigate — together, please bear in mind always together — not only the nature of religion, but also the computer. You know what the computer is? It's a machine; it can programme itself. It can bring about its own computer; the father computer has its own son computer which is better than the father. You don't have to accept this; it's public; it's not something secret, so watch it carefully. That computer can do almost anything that man can do. It can make all your gods, all your theories, your rituals; it's even better at it than you will ever be. So, the computer is coming up in the world; it's going to make your brains something different. You've heard of genetic engineering; they're trying, whether you like it or not, to change your whole behaviour. That is genetic engineering. They are trying to change your way of thinking.

When genetic engineering and the computer meet, what are you? As a human being what are you? Your brains are going to be altered. Your way of behaviour is going to be changed. They may remove fear altogether, remove sorrow, remove all your gods. They're going to; don't fool yourself. It all ends up either in war or in death. This is what is happening in the world actually. Genetic engineering on the one side and the computer on the other, and when they meet, as they're inevitably going to, what are you as a human being? Actually, your brain now is a machine. You are born in India and say: 'I'm an Indian.' You are encased in that. You are a machine. Please don't be insulted. I'm not insulting you. You are a machine which repeats like a computer. Don't imagine there is something divine in you — that would be lovely — something holy that is everlasting. The computer will say that to you too. So, what is becoming of a human being? What's becoming of you?

We have also to enquire — this is a very serious subject, don't agree or disagree, just listen — into what is creation. Not the creation of a baby, that's very simple, or the creation of a new something or other. Invention is totally different from creation. Invention is based on knowledge. The engineers can improve the jet; the movement is based on knowledge and the invention is also based on knowledge. So we must separate invention from creation. This requires your total energy, your capacity to penetrate. Invention is essentially based on knowledge. I improve the clock; I have a new gadget. All invention is based on knowledge, on experience; inventions are inevitably limited because they're based on knowledge. Knowledge being ever limited, inventions must always be limited. In the future there may be no jets, but something else that will go from Delhi to Los Angeles in two hours; that's an invention based on previous knowledge which has been improved step by step, but that's not creation.

So what is creation? So what is life? Life in the tree, life in the little grass — life, not what the scientists invent, but the beginning of life — life, the thing that *lives*? You may kill it, but it's still there in the other. Don't agree or disagree, but see that we are enquiring into the origin of life. We are going to enquire into the *absolute* — something that's really marvellous. It's not a reward; you can't take it home and use it.

What is meditation to you? What is meditation? The word, in common language in the dictionary, means: to ponder over, to think over and to concentrate, to learn to concentrate, not let your brain wander all over the place. Is that what you call meditation? Be simple, be honest. That is what? Every day taking a certain period and going to a room and sitting down quietly for ten minutes or half an hour to meditate? Is meditation concentration, thinking about something very noble? Any conscious effort to meditate is part of your discipline of the office, because you say: If I meditate, I'll have a quiet mind, or I'll enter into another state. The word 'meditation' also means to measure, which means compare. So your meditation becomes mechanical because you are exercising energy to concentrate on a picture, an image, or an idea, and that concentration divides. Concentration is always divisive; you want to concentrate on something, but thought wanders off; then you say you mustn't wander off, and you come back. You repeat that all day long, or for half an hour. Then you come off it and say you have meditated. This meditation is advocated by all the gurus, by all the lay disciples. The Christian idea is: 'I believe in God and I'm sacrificing myself to God; therefore, I pray to save my soul.' Is all this meditation? I know nothing about this kind of meditation; it's like an achievement; if I meditate for half an hour, I feel better. Or is there a totally different kind of meditation? Don't accept anything that the speaker says, at any price. The speaker says that that is not meditation at all. That's merely a process of achievement. If one day you have not been able to concentrate, you take a month and say: 'Yes, I've got it.' That's like a clerk becoming a manager. So is there a different kind of meditation which is not effort, which is not measurement, which is not routine, which is not mechanical? Is there a meditation in which there is no sense of comparison, or in which there is no reward and punishment? Is there any meditation which is not based on thought which is measurement, time, and all that?

How can one explain a meditation that has no measurement, that has no achievement, that doesn't say: 'I'm this, but I'll become that'? 'That' being god or superangel. Is there a meditation which has nothing to do with will—an energy that says: 'I must meditate'? Is there a meditation which has nothing to do with effort at all? The speaker says there is. You don't have to accept it. He may be talking nonsense, but he sees logically that the ordinary meditation is self-hypnosis, deceiving oneself. And, when you stop deceiving, stop all that mechanical process, is there a different kind of meditation? And unfortunately, the speaker says: Yes. But you can't get at it through effort, through giving all your energy to something. It is something that has to be *absolutely silent*. First of all, begin very humbly, very, very humbly and, therefore, very gently and, therefore, no pushing, driving, saying: 'I must do this.' It requires a tremendous sense not only of aloneness, but a sense of— I mustn't describe it to you. I mustn't describe it because then you'll go off on descriptions. If I describe it, the description is not the real. The description of the moon is not the moon, and a painting of the Himalayas is not the Himalayas. So, we'll stop describing. It's for you to play with it, or not play with it, going your own way with your own peculiar achievements through meditation, reward and all the rest of it. So, in meditation which is absolutely no effort, no achievement, no thinking, the brain is quiet; not made quiet by will, by intention, by conclusion and all that nonsense; it is quiet. And, being quiet, it has infinite space. Are you waiting for me to explore? And you will follow what I explain? What kind of people are you?

So, is your brain ever quiet? I'm asking you. Your brain is thinking, fearing, thinking of your office work, of your family, what they will do, your sons, your daughters; thinking, which is time and thought. Is your brain ever *quiet*? Not made quiet by drugs, whiskey and various forms of drugging yourself. You drug yourself when you believe. You drug yourself and say: 'Yes, this is perfectly right, the Buddha has said that, therefore it must be right.' You're drugging yourself all the time; therefore, you have no energy of that kind that demands the penetration of something immense.

So, we're now going back to find out what creation is. What is creation? It has nothing to do with invention. So what is creation, the origin, the beginning? What is life? Tell me what you think of it. What is life? Not going to the office and all the rest of it, sex and children, or no children but sex and so on and so on and so on. What is life? What gives life to that blade of grass in the cement? What is life in us? Not all the things that we go through — power, position, prestige, fame, or no fame, but shame; that's not life; that's part of our mishandling of life. But, what is life?

Why are you listening to me? What makes you, if you are listening at all, listen to the man? What is the motive behind your listening? What do you want? What's your desire? Behind the desire there is a motive. So what is desire? Desire is part of sensation, isn't it? I see this beautiful clock or ugly clock; it's a sensation. The seeing brings about a sensation. From that sensation, thought comes and makes an image of it. That is, I see this clock, rather nice, I would like to have it. The sensation of seeing, then thought coming and making an image of that sensation; at that moment, desire is born. It's very simple.

Is there a brain, your brain, which is not muddied up, muddied by environment, by tradition, by society and all the rest of it? So what is the origin of life? Are you waiting for me to answer it? This is much too serious a subject for you to play with, because we are trying to enquire into something that has no name, no end. I can kill that bird; there is another bird. I can't kill *all* birds; there are too many of them in the world. So, we are enquiring into what makes a bird. What is creation behind all this? Are you waiting for me to describe it, go into it? You want me to go into it? Why

*(From the audience): To understand what creation is.*

Why do you ask that? Because I asked? No description can ever describe the origin. The origin is nameless; the origin is *absolutely quiet*, it's not whirring about making noise. Creation is something that is most holy, that's the most sacred thing in life, and if you have made a mess of your life, change it. Change it today, not tomorrow. If you are uncertain, find out why and be *certain*. If your thinking is not straight, think straight, logically. Unless all that is prepared, all that is settled, you can't enter into this world, into the world of creation.

It ends. *(These two words are hardly audible, breathed rather than spoken.)*

This is the last talk. Do you want to sit together quietly for a while? All right, sirs, sit quietly for a while.